COMPREHENSION INTERVENTION

Small-Group Lessons for The **Primary** Comprehension **Toolkit**

Stephanie Harvey

Anne Goudvis

Judy Wallis

*first*hand
HEINEMANN
DEDICATED TO TEACHERS

DEDICATED TO TEACHERS

*first*hand
An imprint of Heinemann
361 Hanover Street
Portsmouth, NH 03801-3912
firsthand.heinemann.com

Offices and agents throughout the world

©2010 by Stephanie Harvey, Anne Goudvis, and Judy Wallis.
All rights reserved.

No part of this book may be reproduced in any form or by any electronic or
mechanical means, including information storage and retrieval systems, without
permission in writing from the publisher, except by a reviewer, who may quote
brief passages in a review.

'Dedicated to Teachers' is a trademark of Greenwood Publishing Group, Inc.

Cataloguing-in-Publication data for this book is available from
the Library of Congress.

ISBN-10: 0-325-02846-X
ISBN-13: 978-0-325-02846-0

Design and production: Eclipse Publishing Services
Cover photograph: David Stirling

Printed in the United States of America

14 13 12   VP   3 4 5 6

Contents

The small-group sessions in *Comprehension Intervention* reinforce the original lessons in *The Primary Comprehension Toolkit*. The following chart correlates the original Toolkit lesson with its corresponding intervention session(s) and shows the page on which you will find the small-group session.

ASK QUESTIONS

INFER AND VISUALIZE

DETERMINE IMPORTANCE

Summarize and Synthesize

Comprehension Intervention User's Guide

WELCOME TO COMPREHENSION INTERVENTION, a resource of small-group lessons for *The Comprehension Toolkits. The Comprehension Toolkit* and *The Primary Comprehension Toolkit* focus on practices that feature explicit, robust, in-depth comprehension instruction. Successful Toolkit instruction leads to students reading engaging texts at their level, thinking deeply about them, interacting with others, and acquiring knowledge. The Toolkit is founded on several major principles of reading, learning, and achievement. Research (adapted from Allington 2009) indicates that to become proficient readers, students must:

- spend large amounts of time reading and thinking in text they can and want to read;
- have extensive opportunities to respond to their reading through talking, writing, and drawing;
- view reading as a meaningful activity that is personally fulfilling;
- focus on big ideas, issues, and concepts across disciplines; and
- receive explicit instruction in using strategies as tools for decoding and comprehension.

The comprehension lessons in the Toolkits are primarily launch lessons that are designed to be used with the whole class to kick-start kids into wide and effective reading. In fact, they are more than just whole-group lessons. They model practices we teach again and again with a variety of texts, in different contexts, and for many different purposes. We teach these lessons in science, social studies, for research and inquiry projects, in small groups and with individuals. Comprehension instruction in the Toolkits lays a foundation of thinking so that students internalize ways to comprehend what they read and apply strategies in their own independent reading and learning. The whole point of Toolkit comprehension strategy instruction is to move kids toward independence. We view *Comprehension Intervention* as a bridge to that reading independence.

We created *Comprehension Intervention* as a resource to provide additional support to kids who need more time and more explicit instruction to integrate comprehension strategies and use them as tools for learning and understanding. One might ask, why an intervention resource that focuses exclusively on comprehension instruction? The short answer is that there are many programs out there for small-group intervention that stress decoding, fluency, and other aspects of reading, but there are few, if any, that focus intensively on comprehension.

The long answer begins with the conclusions of the final report on Reading First (Gamse, Jacob, Horst, Boulay, and Unlu 2008): "Reading First did not produce a statistically significant impact on student reading comprehension." All that time, money, and effort, and kids apparently didn't get better at what really matters in reading, constructing meaning. So the small-group sessions in *Comprehension Intervention* provide authentic comprehension instruction that engages kids and teaches them to think actively as they read. Now we don't for a minute believe that kids don't need to be taught to decode the words, but surface-structure resources abound. *Comprehension Intervention* fills a void and provides a reading resource that teaches kids to think, to understand, and to use strategies as tools for learning. That, to our way of thinking, is what comprehension is all about.

FROM WHOLE GROUP TO SMALL GROUP

Of late, whole-group instruction has gotten a bad rap. And we understand why. Endless recitation sessions, reams of fill-in-the-blank worksheets, and kids reading the text out loud in unison often characterize whole-group work. And this isn't hyperbole. According to Pianta, Belsky, Houts, and Morrison (2007), students spend about 92% of the school day in their seats listening to the teacher or doing individual seatwork. But whole-group instruction does not have to look like this.

In Toolkit whole-group learning, kids participate in guided discussions designed to get at significant issues, ideas, and concepts that matter. The teacher acts more as a "guide on the side" than a "sage on the stage." Kids do much of the work—interacting with one another and responding throughout the lesson by talking, writing, and drawing. Rich talk about text leads to greater understanding and long-term learning. These active conversations help students transfer their collaborative thinking into their own reading. Discussions about shared texts build a community of learners, thinkers, and communicators who ask questions, debate opinions, build and actively use knowledge, work as a team, and ultimately care about each other and their place in the world.

We emphasize whole-group instruction in *The Comprehension Toolkit* and *The Primary Comprehension Toolkit* for two main reasons. First, we want all kids to engage in the spirited discussions and interactions that characterize Toolkit instruction so they can all contribute their thoughts and ideas to whole-class conversations. Kids in need of additional support should not be pulled out during the whole-class Toolkit lessons. The shared readings in the Toolkit whole-group lessons give all kids the chance to engage, participate, and learn from each other. Secondly, in whole-group Toolkit instruction, kids get the opportunity to practice what they are learning right there in front of the teacher. They are bunched up close on the floor where all are engaged, with each other as well as with the teacher. This proximity allows the teacher to focus on their responses and to adapt instruction accordingly throughout the whole-group lesson. No more teacher doing all of the talking and kids merely staring back! All kids participate together in the active learning process. As the teacher models instruction, the kids turn and talk to one another, jot and draw thinking, and synthesize information.

During much of guided practice in the Toolkit lessons, the kids remain gathered on the floor to practice the task with a partner or on their own as the teacher touches base and confers. After time spent practicing up close with the teacher, the kids go off on their own or in pairs and continue reading and working. During this time, the teacher moves about the room meeting with the kids to support and assess how things are going. The teacher's observations guide the next instructional steps. This is when small groups come in. In short, small-group instruction does not replace whole-group instruction; it enhances it.

RESPONSIVE SMALL-GROUP INSTRUCTION

Children differ. They learn in fits and starts. What works for one may not work for another. For some, it's a matter of time. For others, it's a matter of interest. Some kids take these strategies and run with them after one whole-group Toolkit lesson. Others need additional time, guidance, and practice to internalize comprehension strategies and use them to make sense of what they read. The small-group sessions in *Comprehension Intervention* are specifically designed to support those kids. And small groups work. Pianta et al. (2007) found evidence that "opportunities to learn in small groups, to improve analytical skills, [and] to interact extensively with teachers . . . add depth to students' understanding." But small groups need to be flexible and needs-based so we can meet kids where they are and take them where they need to go.

The small-group reading and thinking strategy sessions in *Comprehension Intervention* are especially useful for kids who find comprehension problematic. We all need a quiver full of strategies to pull out when reading gets tough. Kids who have difficulty with comprehension need even more carefully scaffolded support from the teacher if they are to transfer these strategies to their own reading and thinking and turn them into tools they can use flexibly and at will. Created to follow each Toolkit lesson, the *Comprehension Intervention* small-group sessions target a specific instructional focus, concentrating on critical aspects of the Toolkit's lesson strategy to reinforce kids' understanding, step by step.

Using the language of the Toolkits in a small-group setting, *Comprehension Intervention* approaches each Toolkit strategy lesson in a new way and with new texts, showing kids that they can apply the thinking and strategy language they learned within the whole group to a wide variety of readings.

Responsive instruction is differentiation at its best. *Comprehension Intervention* lays out a framework for effective small-group instruction and builds the following best practices into differentiated instruction.

These small-group sessions provide the perfect opportunity to:

- Scaffold comprehension instruction, providing guidance to kids and instant feedback to teachers
- Zero in on comprehension strategies as tools for understanding
- Provide flexible differentiated instruction based on individual needs
- Focus on key Toolkit goals in need of reinforcement
- Reinforce the strategy language and concepts of the Toolkit lessons
- Extend the time dedicated to guided practice, giving kids opportunities to read and use strategies with text at their level and the teacher right there
- Keep sessions child-focused and fast-paced with kids doing most of the work
- Break down strategy lessons into smaller parts and teach those explicitly
- Use engaging text to promote new learning in the context of real reading
- Match texts to kids' interests and reading levels
- Observe and assess individuals' understanding of specific strategies
- Check children's understanding of a variety of genre included in the Toolkits: nonfiction, poetry, realistic and historical fiction

ASSESSING WHILE TEACHING

Our instruction must match our kids' needs. After a whole-group lesson, we assess children's reading and convene flexible small groups based on these needs. One of the reasons we meet with small groups is so we can readily and seamlessly assess kids' progress. With a small group, we can pay very close attention to exactly what our students are thinking and doing. We can easily hear them read. We can read their Post-its quickly. And we can engage in extended conversations with them—all so we can uncover their thinking as they make sense of text (or not). So when we meet in small intervention groups, it is a 24/7 assessment opportunity. Think of it as a teaching-assessing loop, where we are continuously engaged in formative assessment. By reading students' work and listening to them read and talk, we get a good idea of what to teach next and where each student needs to go.

Comprehension Intervention focuses on ongoing formative assessment while we teach comprehension. At the end of each session, an Assess and Plan section focuses attention on key performance indicators for that session and on what might be done to address them. In the Toolkits, each lesson in each strategy book has an extensive assessment section that gives examples of kids' work accompanied by our analysis. We recommend that as you take kids through the intervention sessions, you frequently refer back to the Reflect and Assess sections of the Toolkit and use the annotated work samples and our commentary as a guide for your own assessment throughout the intervention sessions. In addition, both Toolkit and *Comprehension Intervention* have tools for summative assessment at the end of each unit.

Instructional Settings for *Comprehension Intervention*

Philosophically, it is important that, as teachers, we get to know kids as readers and thinkers. We watch them carefully in an effort to target our instruction to their specific needs. After kids participate in the whole-group Toolkit lesson, we form small groups based on our close observation of kids' work and progress. Our intervention groups stem from what we learn about kids as we instruct them and assess their reading. Some of these intervention groups are classroom-based and led by the classroom teacher. Others occur outside of the classroom with specialists providing the instruction. The *Comprehension Intervention* sessions can be beneficial in the following instructional settings.

Guided reading groups—Sometimes we convene small, flexible, needs-based guided reading groups to reinforce or extend what we have taught in a Toolkit lesson. In a small group, we can carefully guide instruction and gradually release kids as they demonstrate increased independence. These groups may meet two or three times or more frequently, based on kids' needs, to ensure that they are internalizing the Toolkit strategies and using them in their independent reading. These guided reading groups can be taught by the classroom teacher or a specialist.

Tier 2 RTI (Response to Intervention) groups—Tier 2 support is additional, intensive, small-group instruction delivered by the teacher or a reading specialist. Experts suggest that a Tier 2 small-group intervention might span eight to twelve weeks and is considered temporary.

"Tier 2 intervention increases the intensity of instruction…by reducing the size of the group and increasing the duration and frequency of support." (Howard 2009, 71) The best and most effective Tier 2 instruction encourages kids to spend an additional 30 minutes a day reading authentic text at their level and of interest to them, with the teacher providing explicit comprehension instruction. *The Comprehension Intervention* sessions are designed to take about 30 minutes. They break down the original Toolkit instruction into smaller steps, making learning more accessible for Tier 2 students.

Tier 3 RTI groups—Tier 3 increases the instructional intensity further by decreasing the size of the group to either one-on-one or up to three students and increasing the frequency and duration of instruction to two 30-minute daily sessions. (Howard 2009, 79) The sessions in *Comprehension Intervention* are useful because they help teachers continue to break strategy instruction down into smaller steps using a variety of texts and allowing additional time for instruction and practice.

Special education—Kids who are identified for special education and have IEPs (individual education plans) in reading can also benefit from the *Comprehension Intervention* sessions. Whether the kids go to the resource room or the special ed teacher comes into the classroom, the sessions target very specific skills and strategies and build children's comprehension over time. And perhaps best of all, the Toolkit whole-group lessons are ideal for special ed inclusion because they are based on shared readings, which allow for natural differentiation. All kids can participate in the whole-group Toolkit lessons and then have their individual needs met in the small-group intervention sessions.

Other reading support groups: Title 1, after-school tutoring, summer school, and so on—The *Comprehension Intervention* sessions offer opportunities for engaging small groups in real reading and carefully scaffolded instruction in settings outside of the classroom as well as in it. Most of the reading problems that kids demonstrate are comprehension-based, so we need to teach explicitly in a variety of small groups, such as Title 1 reading groups, summer school support, and after-school tutoring.

ORGANIZING FOR *COMPREHENSION INTERVENTION*: IN-CLASS INSTRUCTION

One reason that classroom teachers often shy away from small-group instruction is the need to keep the rest of the class occupied while they concentrate on the small group. Seriously, how can we create thoughtful, independent practice for all of the other kids while we are leading a small group? That is the $64,000 question! And it's not just about keeping kids busy. When loaded up with worksheets and other busy work, kids quickly lose interest, management issues surface, and learning goes south. Active literacy means that kids need to stay busy for sure, but busy with thoughtful work, work that stimulates, challenges, and engages them. Our solution is to take the practices from the Toolkit and set up tasks where kids can read, apply Toolkit strategies, think and question, and add to their knowledge base all on their own. When you are with a small group, the other kids can:

- Interact with images, placing Post-its of their thoughts and questions on the image and talking about it with a partner
- Read text, interacting with it by jotting their thinking and drawing what they are learning
- Listen to someone read, jotting down what they learned and what they wonder, sharing that with the reader
- Watch streaming video and write and draw questions, connections, and other thoughts while watching
- Refer to anchor charts that were created during a Toolkit lesson and use them to guide a variety of responses
- Write and draw their own books, using the many nonfiction texts and images in the room as mentor texts
- Use nonfiction features in their writing and drawing to help readers better understand what they have written
- Create posters to demonstrate learning
- Research topics related to ongoing content area units
- Create group murals of topics from the content areas that the class is studying
- Respond to and illustrate their thoughts about poetry
- Extend their learning by asking questions and searching for answers
- Go online to answer questions and find information at approved sites
- Work with several others in inquiry circles or literature circles
- Read text simply for the sake of it!!
- Participate in any other interactive process that nudges kids to think, learn, and understand

ORGANIZING FOR *COMPREHENSION INTERVENTION:* OUT-OF-CLASS INSTRUCTION

Pullout groups solve the challenge of keeping the other kids busy but create another one: How do you keep intervention instruction consistent and coherent with the foundation whole-class Toolkit lesson the kids have already experienced? This is especially difficult if another teacher or a specialist is in charge of small-group reinforcement. *Comprehension Intervention* is designed to make the transition from whole class to small group as seamless as possible. The *Comprehension Intervention* objectives and instructional language match and in some cases extend the Toolkit lessons. Pullout teachers who pick up *Comprehension Intervention* sessions for the first time and are unfamiliar with the Toolkit will still be using the same terminology, the same teaching language, and the same learning prompts with which the classroom teacher introduced the original Toolkit lesson. *Comprehension Intervention* also provides an avenue for more effective communication between the regular education teacher and the pullout specialist since the intervention sessions are designed to follow up the whole-class Toolkit lesson. The conversation between teachers can focus more explicitly on instruction because kids are working on the same strategies both in and out of the classroom. In addition, the Assess and Plan section at the end of each intervention session provides specific recommendations that can be used to coordinate with other members of a student's instructional team.

GETTING STARTED WITH *COMPREHENSION INTERVENTION*

The *Comprehension Intervention* small-group sessions are designed to follow the whole-group lessons in the Toolkits. They are effective for kids who need additional support. There is a fine line, however, between convening a small group too soon and waiting too long to reteach and reinforce the lesson.

Assessing to Plan Instruction—Before deciding on and planning to engage kids in a small intervention group, we assess them to determine if they need additional scaffolded instruction and to design that instruction. To do this, we:

- Observe children's efforts and participation during the guided, collaborative, and independent practice part of the whole-class Toolkit lesson
- Read and analyze children's responses from the whole-group lesson as well as any follow-up lessons
- Listen in on their conversations as they practice collaboratively and independently
- Listen to them read and talk to them about their reading
- Confer with them individually to assess their understanding and make sure we understand the thinking behind their written and drawn responses
- Notice how effectively they use the strategies we have taught

Based on our assessment of how purposefully and effectively students use strategies to understand what they read, we convene small intervention groups for those who need more instructional time and practice to access and use reading and thinking strategies. They frequently fall into the categories mentioned earlier: flexible guided reading groups, Tier 2 or Tier 3 RTI groups, and a variety of other reading support groups, including special education.

Gathering Appropriate Texts—We have said it before: Half of our success as teachers is getting the right texts into kids' hands. The right book or article can ignite kids' interest, launching them into a lifetime of reading. Nonfiction is the most accessible genre. Stuffed with information of every type, it is a powerful way into reading. Packed with illustrations, graphs, charts, photos, maps, and so forth, nonfiction lures the kids to jump in and explore the real world.

Although each *Comprehension Intervention* session provides suggestions for texts that are appropriate for teaching the particular lesson strategy, you will want to have an arsenal of surefire texts at hand. As we gather text for small-group comprehension instruction, we make sure that we collect a variety of nonfiction text at different levels on a wide range of topics. Kids who find reading a challenge often gravitate to the topics that they are interested in, and nonfiction frequently fills the bill. We take great care to match students with text they are interested in at their reading level. When kids are reading at their own level, they devour books and effectively use strategies not only to understand but also to think beyond the text. Above all, we make sure to build in a great deal of time for kids to actually read text at their level, so they can develop as readers and become lifelong learners.

The Toolkit lessons are primarily centered on nonfiction. Kids in small intervention groups will have had exposure to the nonfiction text in the original Toolkit lessons. For the *Comprehension Intervention* sessions, we encourage you to choose text that will fire up your kids and to match it to the reading level of most of the group. Since intervention groups average from 20–30 minutes in length, the text must be short. We offer several text possibilities in each of the *Comprehension Intervention* sessions, but you also might want to consider the following sources:

- Articles from ***Keep Reading: A Source Book of Short Text*** in *The Primary Comprehension Toolkit* and articles from ***The Source Book of Short Text*** in *The Comprehension Toolkit* for grades 3–6. In addition to the lesson texts, both of these source books include lots of additional practice texts. In the grades 3–6 *Source Book*, pages 92–135 include texts on a variety of levels and a myriad of topics from magic to the Tour de France. In *Keep Reading*, the primary source book, pages 50–137 include articles at different levels on nature, weather, sports, and a variety of other topics.

- Articles from **Toolkit Texts**. At www.comprehensiontoolkit.com or at www.heinemann.com, you can order our *Toolkit Texts*, three volumes of short nonfiction articles on a universe of topics. We have arranged these texts by "grade level." You can choose from grades 2–3, grades 4–5, or grades 6–7, whatever meets your kids' needs.

- Additionally, seek out articles and books that relate to the content of the Toolkit lesson text or whatever social studies or science unit currently engages your class. Once kids whet their appetite for a topic, they can hardly wait to read more about it. Magazines for kids and online sources are all just a click away. We have extensive bibliographies in the Toolkits to help you find just the right text for your kids. Check out the bibliographies beginning on page 139 in *Keep Reading* in *The Primary Comprehension Toolkit* and on page 127 in *Extend and Investigate* in *The Comprehension Toolkit*, grades 3–6.

- Listings of websites containing a wealth of information and more articles begin on page 154 in *Keep Reading* in *The Primary Toolkit* and on page 138 in *Extend and Investigate* in the grades 3–6 Toolkit.

- Don't forget the books and topics you love! Passion is contagious and your kids will likely hop on board as you share text you care about.

THE INTERVENTION SESSIONS

In *Comprehension Intervention*, we have broken down the original Toolkit lessons into smaller chunks of instruction to make them more explicit and accessible. For instance, if a Toolkit lesson has three goals, we may have three separate intervention sessions to help kids meet these goals. But the intervention sessions are designed to be flexible and to target very specific comprehension needs. Sometimes our kids need all of the sessions on a specific strategy, other times one or two suffice. Kids come to the intervention sessions with some experience with the strategies that were the focus of the whole-group lesson, but our intervention highlights and revisits specific language and thinking behaviors that need additional reinforcement and practice.

Each intervention session corresponds to a specific Toolkit lesson and goals. Based on the complexity of the Toolkit lesson, we have created small-group sessions to reinforce specific parts of the Toolkit lesson. For some of the Toolkit lessons, we offer one intervention session. For others we offer as many as three or four. These multiple sessions are designated by the notation *a*, *b*, *c*, and so forth, so small-group sessions 4a and 4b are both companions to Toolkit Lesson 4. You are free to teach any or all of these based on your kids' needs.

SUMMATIVE ASSESSMENT

We have created guidelines for a summative assessment conference to target how effectively children are using the strategies as tools for understanding as they read, listen, and view. Once kids have completed all of the intervention sessions in a specific strategy and have had lots of time to practice, we suggest you use our Reading Conference protocol and recording form. This conference provides an opportunity for a more formal assessment of how your kids are using strategies to understand what they read.

SESSION WALK-THROUGH

Comprehension Intervention's four-part session supports a gradual release of responsibility from teacher to student.

1. Build Background, Word and Concept Knowledge

2. Teach/Model   **3.** Guide/Support Practice   **4.** Wrap Up

Each small-group session is identified by a numeral that matches the Toolkit lesson it follows, and, when there are multiple small-group interventions for one Toolkit lesson, a letter. So Session 2a is the first lesson for Toolkit Lesson 2; Session 2b is the second.

The first page of every session supports planning for instruction.

- **Session Goals** restate key objectives from the Toolkit launch lesson.
- **Text Matters** explains the attributes of text appropriate to this lesson and provides examples.
- **Considerations for Planning** discusses the teaching focus and key understandings as well as noting materials teachers will need to prepare for the session.

Like the Toolkit lessons, these sessions include both Teaching Moves, the step-by-step teaching procedure, and Teaching Language, the words you may use to teach key concepts to kids.

Build Background, Word and Concept Knowledge begins the session, and the teacher may:

- Connect and engage kids with the strategy
- Ask, "What do you think you know about _____?" to evaluate background content knowledge
- Provide a brief text or picture walk to preview key concepts and vocabulary
- Anticipate the hurdles that content, vocabulary, genre knowledge, decoding issues, and the like may present and troubleshoot accordingly

In **Teach/Model**, the teacher:

- Previews the text with kids
- Provides a brief read-aloud or think-aloud
- Explains the strategy and demonstrates how to use it

Throughout **Guide/Support Practice**, kids and teacher work together on the strategy.

- Kids and teacher read a section together; kids turn and talk; and all practice using the strategy.
- Kids read a section and use the strategy independently; teacher listens in and confers as needed.
- Kids whisper-read and use the strategy; teacher listens in, monitoring and coaching fluency and strategy use.

In **Wrap Up**, the final part of the teaching sequence, kids share and consolidate their knowledge.

- Kids share out.
- Kids and teacher summarize what was learned.
- Kids create or add to an anchor chart with the teacher.
- Kids reread for fluency practice.
- Kids go off to use the strategy with their own independent texts.

Teach/Model

TEACHING MOVES

- Explain that **reading involves reading all the features** the author includes to increase understanding.

- Think aloud as you investigate the visual and text features students will encounter in the text. **Create a *Feature/Purpose* chart** to show how each feature is a source of information for the reader.

- **Model how you notice and name the features.** The language used will offer kids a way to anchor their own inner conversation when they read independently.

- **Invite kids' observations.** Ask students to turn and talk as you share your thinking. Listen to kids' comments for insights about their understanding.

TEACHING LANGUAGE

. . . Today we will work together to learn more about these features and their purposes. Reading involves reading all the features the author includes, so let's investigate!

. . . Let's preview the text together, looking at the features. I want you to listen and watch me as I think about the features and their purposes. To help us keep track of all the ways the author supports and expands our thinking through the features, let's record them on a chart.

. . . Let's begin . . . Here is a photograph. Let's think about why the author might have included it. (Continue to explore the features, having kids turn and talk as you notice and name the features.)

. . . We can be sure when an author includes a text feature, we should say, "Wow, this is probably important!"

Feature	Purpose
photograph	to show something
label	to tell about the photograph or drawing

Guide/Support Practice

TEACHING MOVES

- During the guided practice, **involve students in discussing the features.** This will lay the groundwork for reading the text in the next session.

- During this session, **see if students are able to name a feature and its purpose.** Celebrate kids' successful attempts, adding any additional information that might make a strong model.

- As students continue through the remainder of the book, stop to **add features and purposes to the chart**, furnishing or co-constructing the name and purpose when necessary.

- Students will use the chart as support when they **read the text in the next session.**

TEACHING LANGUAGE

. . . It's time for you to help me. Look at the next two pages. Turn and talk about any features you see, and consider why the author might have included them—what their purposes might be. When you talk, it might sound like this.

- This is an illustration . . . I think the author might have included it right here to help me . . .
- Here's a label. Wow, this really helps me because I wasn't sure what that was!

(Add features to the chart as they are identified, scaffolding kids as necessary with terms and purposes.)

Teaching Tip
Use consistent language when naming features. While terms vary and are all correct, select the one you will use and stick to it.

Wrap Up

TEACHING MOVES

- Have students **reread the *Feature/Purpose* chart** for this text. You may have kids take turns reading individually or use the chart as shared reading.

- Ask kids to review and **summarize what they learned** in this session.

TEACHING LANGUAGE

. . . Let's review our *Feature/Purpose* chart for this text. This chart is great because it will help us as we read the text next time we meet.

. . . You did a good job today! Let's close by having you share your new learning. Who can summarize why the features are so important for us to note as readers? Name some of the features you have learned and the purposes they serve.

Each session ends with **Assess and Plan**, a section that supports daily progress monitoring with strategy-specific suggestions for reviewing student work, assessing students' thinking and accomplishment of session goals, and determining the need for additional practice.

A PLUG FOR READING!

Often when kids are identified as needing special help in reading, they are pulled out of the room during class reading time. What's wrong with this picture? Children who need additional support in reading should get *more* time with reading instruction, not less. They should participate fully in classroom reading instruction as well as receiving additional small-group support, either in or out of class. Kids' strategy knowledge is cumulative. As they participate in both whole-group and small-group comprehension lessons, they acquire a repertoire of strategies to use as tools for understanding. They integrate comprehension strategies as a part of their entire thinking process.

But collaborative whole-group and differentiated small-group instruction alone aren't enough. To get better at reading, kids need to log a lot of reading time in text they can and want to read. The less developed the reader, the more reading time he or she needs! Too often, the more students struggle with reading, the less time they actually get to read, partly because they are in text that is too hard for them and frequently because they are spending time on isolated skill-and-drill worksheets that provide no opportunities to read and learn. Allington (2009) suggests that students who are "behind grade level" in reading need to spend up to three times as much time reading as their grade-level peers. Kids get better at reading by reading! And reading makes them smarter, too. So give all of our kids lots of time to read, but give even more reading time to kids who need additional support. A nose in a good book is the best intervention of all!

REFERENCES

Allington, R.L. 2009. *What Really Matters in Response to Intervention: Research-Based Designs.* Boston: Pearson.

Gamse, B.C., Jacob, R.T., Horst, M., Boulay, B., and Unlu, F. 2008. Reading First Impact Study Final Report (Report No. NCEE 2009–4038). Washington, DC: National Center for Education Evaluation and Regional Assistance, Institute of Education Sciences, U. S. Department of Education.

Howard, M. 2009. *RTI from All Sides: What Every Teacher Needs to Know.* Portsmouth, NH: Heinemann.

Pianta, R.C., Belsky, J., Houts, R., and Morrison, F. 2007. "Opportunities to Learn in America's Elementary Classrooms." *Science* 315: 1795–1796.

Monitor Comprehension

When readers monitor their comprehension, they keep track of their thinking as they read, listen, and view. They notice when the text makes sense and when it doesn't. They distinguish between what the text is about and what it makes them think about. Primary-grade kids are always thinking about what they hear, see, and (if they can) read. They are noticing, wondering, making connections, and making judgments all the time. When they monitor their comprehension, they use that awareness to steer their thinking as they enter texts. They expect to interact with the pictures, the features, the words, and the ideas. Rather than simply retelling the story, kids need to go beyond retelling to merge their thinking with the text. This is how they come up with the "big ideas." So we focus on teaching kids not just to retell, but to think about the words, the pictures, the features, and the ideas that spring from the text. They stay on track when they talk, draw, and write about their thinking. By interacting with the text and with each other, they gain understanding.

> *In planning effective intervention for developing readers, the most critical fact is matching the reader with texts they can actually read.*
> (Allington, 2009)

Companion to...

The Primary Comprehension Toolkit
Lesson 1: Think about the Text

Leave Tracks of Your Thinking

In *The Primary Comprehension Toolkit* Lesson 1, students respond to a class read-aloud by writing and drawing what the text makes them think about. This companion session for Lesson 1 offers students the opportunity to read and think about another text in a small-group setting, using Post-its to leave tracks of their thinking right in their text.

TEXT MATTERS

Selecting an interesting text that kids will enjoy is important when we teach students to notice and pay attention to their thinking. Texts that invite connections and offer something to wonder about increase student engagement. In addition, it is essential to select a text that students *can* read. Matching kids to an accessible text is critical.

Short books like *The Seasons of Arnold's Apple Tree* by Gail Gibbons and articles like "Shadows" in *Toolkit Texts: Grades 2–3* and "The Grizzly Bear" in *Keep Reading* work well for this session. They offer topics and information that will motivate kids to pay attention to what they are thinking as they read.

CONSIDERATIONS FOR PLANNING

Look through the text you've selected to identify concepts or words that might be unfamiliar. Consider how you might introduce the ideas or vocabulary so that the students spend their energy focusing on meaning.

Consider ways to scaffold and model to support students' success in reading strategically and tracking their thinking.

Students will need Post-its for this session.

SESSION GOALS

We want students to:

- develop an awareness of their thinking as they read, listen, and view.
- leave tracks of their thinking by drawing and writing.

Build Background, Word and Concept Knowledge

TEACHING MOVES

- **Engage students by helping them connect** with the text. Introduce the text in a way that orients kids to the text and provides access to any unfamiliar concepts.

- **Make the text preview interactive,** inviting students to share their ideas and impressions about the text. Celebrate thinking by noticing and naming what they do.

- **Emphasize what kids are thinking.** If the text is nonfiction, ask kids what they know about the topic. If the book is a story or narrative, tell the kids a bit about the story and check to see if it reminds them of any personal experiences.

- **Point out words and concepts** that might be unfamiliar to students. This scaffolding during the preview will allow readers to focus on thinking.

TEACHING LANGUAGE

. . . I have selected a text for us to read today. Remember how important *your* thinking is as you read! Let's look at the (cover, picture). What are *you* thinking? What do you notice?

. . . What do you know about _____ (the topic)? When we read, we want to think about what we already know about _____.

. . . Let's look at a few of the words the author uses. Some of these may be unfamiliar to you, so we will take a look at them together. That way, when you read, you'll already know what the word means and you can think about the ideas in the text.

. . . That is good thinking! What you just noticed will help you as you read.

Teach/Model

- Explain that **reading involves thinking.**

- Briefly read aloud, modeling how you think as you read and make notes that leave tracks of your thinking. Show how to **record or draw thinking on a Post-it.**

- **Use language that kids can "borrow"** when it is time for them to respond using their own Post-its. That language might include . . .
  - This makes me think of . . .
  - I wonder . . .
  - This reminds me . . .

- **Invite students to turn and talk** as you stop to share your thinking.

- After students talk about their thinking, **have them try jotting their thinking on a Post-it.**

- **After several demonstrations,** check to be sure kids know and understand what they are to do.

Teaching Tip

Since there is a high correlation between reading engagement and comprehension, be sure to build in success. If you see a text is too difficult, provide greater support through shared, rather than guided, reading, and select an easier text for the next session.

. . . Today we will notice and pay careful attention to our thinking as we read. Reading is not just about the words; reading is about what we think about our reading. I'm going to teach you what that thinking sounds and looks like as we read.

. . . One of the ways we pay close attention to our reading is by stopping to think and then writing or drawing our thinking on a Post-it. For example, when I read this part, it makes me think about . . . . Watch how I write and draw that on a Post-it to help me remember what I was thinking when I read that part.

. . . What were you thinking when I read that part?

. . . Let's turn and talk about what you were thinking. When we talk about what we think about a book or text, we are likely to understand it better.

. . . How can you remember that thinking you just shared? Great! Write or draw what you were thinking on a Post-it.

. . . Here is some thinking language we can use . . .
  - This makes me think of . . .
  - I wonder . . .
  - This reminds me . . .

Guide/Support Practice

TEACHING MOVES

- **Do at least one more section together.**
  Look for evidence of confusion so you can offer an additional demonstration as necessary.

- If students show understanding, **have them read on.** Guided practice is a perfect time to differentiate support. Unlike shared reading, we now offer support at the point of need.

- Explain that they will **read in a whisper voice and share their thinking** when you are nearby to listen. Encourage kids to read silently except when you listen in. If they aren't ready to read silently, have them read softly.

- **Move around the group** quickly to determine which students need extra support and to uncover any confusion. Stop the group only if you see several kids are confused.

- **Notice when a student isn't reading,** and provide support by reading together. Some kids will need an additional model to write a Post-it. Find a place to stop and write one together.

- Students may need extra support to share their thinking, so it helps to **have some prompts ready:**
  - I'm thinking . . .
  - An idea I have about this . . .
  - I'm wondering . . .

- Remind kids to **write or draw their thinking** on Post-its as they read.

TEACHING LANGUAGE

. . . Let's share the reading of this next part.

. . . Now that you've finished this part, take one of the Post-its and draw or write what you are thinking. Do you remember some of the things you can write? (If no one volunteers, offer a prompt, but only one at a time. Give students a chance to reflect and think of something that they might draw or write.)

. . . Talk about what you wrote. (Assess to be sure students understand. If they do, let them continue.)

. . . Good! I see that Josh has written . . . (Select and celebrate things students have written that offer models.)

. . . Now it's time for you to read on your own. I will be listening to each of you. When I am nearby, I will ask you to "whisper read" (demonstrate) and think aloud when you think of something to write or draw on your Post-it. It might sound like this: "This reminds me of . . ."

. . . Remember that thinking is an important part of reading! Write or draw your thinking on Post-its as you read. (If the text is too long for one reading, tell students where they should stop.)

Teaching Tip

Support for writing or drawing on the Post-it may be needed. Sometimes teachers help by jotting something on another Post-it as a model. Other times, the teacher actually prompts the thinking and records it for the student.

Wrap Up

TEACHING MOVES

- **Have kids share** their Post-its. This is an effective and efficient way to assess both fluency and comprehension.

- **Create an anchor chart** that records language that celebrates students' thinking and will help remind students of what readers do to track their thinking.

- Students should each have an independent book they are reading. **Connect what they have done** in the small group by offering them Post-its to use for recording their thinking in their independent book.

TEACHING LANGUAGE

. . . Quickly find a part where you put a Post-it. Read the part and the Post-it you wrote. Who wants to start us off?

. . . Who can explain the important work we did today? (If students need support, offer it. It is important to debrief and summarize.)

. . . Let's make an anchor chart to help us remember our thinking language. (Prompt students to recall the thinking language they used.)

Things We Recorded on Our Post-its

- I'm thinking . . .
- It reminded me . . .
- Why did . . . ?
- I wonder what . . .
- An idea from the text
- Wow!

. . . You each have an independent book you are reading. I'll give you some Post-its so you can practice recording your thinking in your own books.

ASSESS AND PLAN

How did students' Post-its show evidence of their thinking?
Look for evidence and consider whether reteaching is necessary.
Consider both the quality and quantity of what students write and
draw. You may want to scribe students' thoughts initially and continue
to demonstrate how to write and draw thinking. Extend the session to
a second day if necessary.

Was the text level appropriate for students? If not, why?
If the text was not a good match, select an easier or a more challenging
text for the next session. Readers need to spend most of their time in
accessible texts.

What did students find easy or challenging?
Consider your observation of students' reading, questions, and need
for support when you are planning. Often these observations can be
used as teaching points in the next session.

Were there any students who would benefit from extra help?
Plan to confer with any reader who might need extra support. Done
quickly, it will help the reader accelerate much more quickly.

**What insights might you gain from the classroom teacher or others
who work with the students?**
Plan to check in regularly with others. The more coordination and
collaboration, the better it is for the students.

Preview Features in a Text

Part of inviting children to notice is helping them see what kind of things might be noticed and to name the things being noticed. (Johnston, 2004)

Companion to . . .

The Primary Comprehension Toolkit Lesson 2: Notice and Think about Nonfiction Features

In *The Primary Comprehension Toolkit* Lesson 2, students explore nonfiction features in a variety of texts and construct a class chart of features and their purposes. The two sessions supporting Lesson 2 offer students the opportunity to think about features in a selected text. In this session, they make a *Feature/Purpose* chart specific to the text they will read in the next session.

TEXT MATTERS

Gather a variety of texts with features kids can explore and think about: photographs, illustrations, captions, bold print, and labels. These are the first features we teach young readers to notice and use in gaining meaning.

Also select a short text kids can read, so you can show them how to preview the features. "The Three Goats," "The City," "Prairie Dog Homes," and "Kids at Play" in *Keep Reading* have features kids can explore and use in strategic ways. So do articles from *Time for Kids* and *National Geographic* included in *The Primary Comprehension Toolkit*.

Be sure to select a text that is well suited for your particular group. The number of features will vary. Selecting a text with too many features may overwhelm some groups.

SESSION GOALS

We want students to:

- notice the visual and text features of nonfiction and understand that they signal importance.
- recognize that the visual and text features have a purpose.

CONSIDERATIONS FOR PLANNING

Look through the text you have selected. Plan how you will scaffold and model how to access the visual and text features. This session focuses on previewing the features, preparing students to read the text in the next session.

In addition to the text students will read, gather other good examples of features so students see a range of possibilities.

If possible, display and refer to the class *Feature/Purpose* chart from *The Primary Comprehension Toolkit* Lesson 2 (the chart with visual examples of each feature).

Build Background, Word and Concept Knowledge

- **Engage students by showing them texts** with a variety of visual and text features. (Selection will be based on the group's unique needs.) Tell students in a general way (you will explore in depth later) that the author's purpose for adding features is always to help readers better understand the text, information, and concepts.

- **Be sure to "name" the features.** The language you use in an incidental way will be important as you continue to investigate more explicitly how features support readers and their evolving understanding. The more kids hear and use the language of reading, the better readers they become.

- **Introduce the text kids will read.** Ask them to name some of the features and share what they know about the topic.

- **Preview words and concepts** that might be unfamiliar. Often specialized vocabulary in informational text presents challenges for students. When you introduce words, be sure to link them to the larger concepts and ideas in the text. This helps students see the relationship of words, concepts, and features.

. . . I am eager to show you the text I have selected for us to read today. It is nonfiction, and it gives us some great information. We can learn a lot of information from the print and photographs (or illustrations).

. . . First let's look at some features in other texts. (Show examples in several texts.) Notice how this photograph offers us a close look at . . . This text includes a diagram of . . . This illustration labels the parts of a . . .

. . . Today you will have a chance to read a text about _____ (topic). Let's look through the text to identify some of the features the author has included. (Support kids to name the features.)

. . . What do you already know about _____ (topic)? Turn and talk.

. . . I want to show you some important words the author uses. Authors often use special words related to the ideas in the text. Since the ideas may be new to us, we may not know the words. Let's look at this word, for example . . . . And here is another interesting word. Let's see how the author uses it . . . .

Teach/Model

- Explain that **reading involves reading all the features** the author includes to increase understanding.

- Think aloud as you investigate the visual and text features students will encounter in the text. **Create a *Feature/Purpose* chart** to show how each feature is a source of information for the reader.

- **Model how you notice and name the features.** The language used will offer kids a way to anchor their own inner conversation when they read independently.

- **Invite kids' observations.** Ask students to turn and talk as you share your thinking. Listen to kids' comments for insights about their understanding.

. . . Today we will work together to learn more about these features and their purposes. Reading involves reading all the features the author includes, so let's investigate!

. . . Let's preview the text together, looking at the features. I want you to listen and watch me as I think about the features and their purposes. To help us keep track of all the ways the author supports and expands our thinking through the features, let's record them on a chart.

. . . Let's begin . . . Here is a photograph. Let's think about why the author might have included it. (Continue to explore the features, having kids turn and talk as you notice and name the features.)

. . . We can be sure when an author includes a text feature, we should say, "Wow, this is probably important!"

Feature	Purpose
photograph	to show something
label	to tell about the photograph or drawing

Guide/Support Practice

- During the guided practice, **involve students in discussing the features.** This will lay the groundwork for reading the text in the next session.

- During this session, **see if students are able to name a feature and its purpose.** Celebrate kids' successful attempts, adding any additional information that might make a strong model.

- As students continue through the remainder of the book, stop to **add features and purposes to the chart,** furnishing or co-constructing the name and purpose when necessary.

- Students will use the chart as support when they **read the text in the next session.**

. . . It's time for you to help me. Look at the next two pages. Turn and talk about any features you see, and consider why the author might have included them—what their purposes might be. When you talk, it might sound like this.

- This is an illustration . . . I think the author might have included it right here to help me . . .
- Here's a label. Wow, this really helps me because I wasn't sure what that was!

(Add features to the chart as they are identified, scaffolding kids as necessary with terms and purposes.)

Teaching Tip

Use consistent language when naming features. While terms vary and are all correct, select the one you will use and stick to it.

Wrap Up

- Have students **reread the *Feature/Purpose* chart** for this text. You may have kids take turns reading individually or use the chart as shared reading.

- Ask kids to review and **summarize what they learned** in this session.

. . . Let's review our *Feature/Purpose* chart for this text. This chart is great because it will help us as we read the text next time we meet.

. . . You did a good job today! Let's close by having you share your new learning. Who can summarize why the features are so important for us to note as readers? Name some of the features you have learned and the purposes they serve.

ASSESS AND PLAN

How did students' language show evidence of their learning and understanding of features and their purposes?

Look for evidence of understanding and determine how much review might be necessary before the students read the text in the next session. Since this session includes challenging concepts, some review will likely be important.

Did the text seem appropriate for students? If not, why?

Evaluate the appropriateness of the text. If it was not easily accessible to students, you might want to begin again with another text on the same topic for the next session.

Which features did students find easy or challenging? Did any of the students seem confused?

Consider your observation of students as they turned and talked and summarized. Plan to give any reader who might need extra support opportunities to look at and talk about some additional examples.

How can you coordinate with others who work with the students?

Since visual and text features are an important part of content-area study, be sure to let science, social studies, and math teachers know what students are learning. The *Feature/Purpose* chart from this session can be typed and shared. Students may use it as a text to read and reference as needed.

> *When readers interact with the text, they are more apt to stay on top of meaning as they read.*
> (Harvey and Goudvis, 2007)

Integrate Information from Features

This session picks up where the previous one leaves off. Students read the text and integrate information from the features.

Companion to . . .

The Primary Comprehension Toolkit
Lesson 2: Notice and Think about Nonfiction Features

TEXT MATTERS

We continue using the text from the previous session.

CONSIDERATIONS FOR PLANNING

Look through the text to review the visual and text features and students' responses to them. Questions you might ask yourself in planning for this session include:

- How confident did the students seem in using the language of the features?
- Did students grasp the understanding that the features signal important information?
- Did students see the connection between a feature and its purpose?
- What features presented the most difficulty?

Be sure to consider how you will monitor not only students' actual reading of the text but also their use and integration of the features for increased understanding and engagement.

Post the *Feature/Purpose* chart that you created with the kids in the previous session, or have typed copies for students to use.

SESSION GOALS

We want students to:
- notice the visual and text features of nonfiction and understand that they signal importance.
- recognize that the visual and text features have a purpose.

Build Background, Word and Concept Knowledge

TEACHING MOVES

- Engage students in a very quick **review of the** *Feature/Purpose* **chart** they made in Session 2a. If you have typed the chart, offer each student a copy to read as a shared text. If not, use the group chart to review.

- **Listen for the "names" of the features.** Strive for consistency so that students create shared language around the features.

- **If any vocabulary needs to be reviewed,** do it quickly, either pointing to the word within the text or jotting it on a dry-erase board.

TEACHING LANGUAGE

. . . I can hardly wait to start reading the text we explored for features and their purposes! Before we begin, however, let's look over the chart we made. Who wants to start us off by sharing one of the features and its purpose? (Continue until all have been reviewed.)

. . . I really liked the way you "named" the features and then told us why the author included them.

. . . Let's also consider some of the new words we explored. Those will be important as you read today.

Teach/Model

TEACHING MOVES

- **Remind the students** that they built good background in the preview and discussion of the features. Reinforce that reading nonfiction involves paying close attention not only to the text, but also to all the features.

- **Do a very short model** so students recall and use their learning from the previous session. As you model, review or demonstrate with a feature that might be challenging for kids. You might discuss information learned from it or review its purpose.

- **Check students' understanding** quickly, asking what they notice.

TEACHING LANGUAGE

. . . Before we start reading, let's talk about what you already know about the text from our preview of the vocabulary and features.

. . . I will read a little of the text to get you started. Watch how I learn information from the features as I read. (Model quickly, but use precise language to show kids how they can learn information from visual and text features.)

. . . Listen as I read the text . . . I am going to stop here because there is a (photograph). It shows . . . This helps me understand . . . (Keep the model brief.)

. . . What did you notice me doing as I read?

Guide/Support Practice

- **Have students read on.** They may read either softly or silently, depending on their development.

- During the guided practice, **offer support as needed.** Be sure to prioritize your support, listening in on the students who seem less secure.

- **Move about the group to listen in** to individual students.

- **Listen for:**
  - **phrasing and fluency** (phrasing will often reveal understanding because the reading sounds natural and expressive)
  - **accuracy** (check to be sure students are able to read the text)
  - **thinking** as they share the inner conversation
  - **connections** to and **integration** of the information

. . . It's time for you to read. I will be listening as you read. Be sure to use your whisper voice, but also be sure you let me hear your thinking. You will read along and when you see a visual or text feature, you will stop and let me hear your inner conversation. All set? Any questions?

> **Teaching Tip**
> Coach students only as needed, offering "just enough" scaffolding. Too much support will mask what readers can do as they problem solve.

Wrap Up

- Have students **look back at the *Feature/ Purpose* chart** they made for the text. Have them share how the features enhanced their reading and understanding.

- Be sure to **celebrate the readers' contributions** and reinforce when they make good connections.

. . . Let's look back at our *Feature/Purpose* chart for this text. Share some of the features you found and how those features helped you gain a better understanding of the topic.

. . . Great connections! Did you hear that? When you see a _____, it helps you . . .

. . . Now turn and talk. Share a feature that was particularly helpful to you—one where you were able to say, "This must really be important to remember!"

. . . You did a good job today!

ASSESS AND PLAN

How did students' reading show evidence of their understanding of features and their purposes?

Look for evidence in the "inner conversation" students shared and note how they learned from text and visual features.

Was the text appropriate for students? If not, how will you plan to offer students a second, more appropriate text?

Consider texts that might be good for follow-up and offer additional practice.

Which features did students share at the end? What features might you need to review or reteach?

If students did not mention some features, plan to incorporate those in a future session. Remember, there will always be opportunities for review of things you have previously taught.

What additional practice might be necessary?

Consider creating a box or basket of texts students might select from for additional practice. Include a copy of the *Feature/Purpose* chart.

> *I reflect on what children say and do, consider the big picture, and think about where it makes sense to go next.* (Miller, 2008)

Explore Visual and Text Features

In *The Primary Comprehension Toolkit* Lesson 3, students explore a variety of texts to compile their own books about nonfiction features.

This companion session offers students more time and support to explore features in selected texts, add to a chart of features and purposes, and differentiate between visual and text features.

Companion to . . .

The Primary Comprehension Toolkit
Lesson 3: Explore Nonfiction
Features

TEXT MATTERS

Gather a variety of books and magazines with visual features (photographs, illustrations, drawings, charts, graphs) and text features (bold print, captions, titles, headings) for students to explore. Be sure to consider students' ages and needs as you select the features. Limit the number and types of features accordingly.

Select a short text with both visual and text features for students to read. Articles such as "The Bald Eagle" and "The Country" in *Keep Reading* and "Rock Secrets" in *Toolkit Texts: Grades 2–3* have information-rich features. Select a text that reinforces features already explored or contains additional ones.

For independent reading, provide plenty of books with strong visual and text features, such as *The Honey Makers* by Gail Gibbons and *Freight Train* by Donald Crews.

CONSIDERATIONS FOR PLANNING

During this session, we add to students' previous understanding by differentiating between *visual features* and *text features*. We show kids how both types of features contribute to understanding.

Have on hand the *Feature/Purpose* chart and the text from the previous session.

You may want to write the names of the features on cards for kids to sort.

SESSION GOALS

We want students to:

- pay attention to both visual and text features and become aware of the difference between them.
- understand the purpose of features is to give readers more information and a more complete understanding.

Build Background, Word and Concept Knowledge

TEACHING MOVES

- Engage students in a quick **review of the** *Feature/Purpose* **chart.**

- **Introduce the terms** *visual features* **and** *text features.* Show examples in the text from the previous session.

- Have kids **think about the features they have studied and sort them** into *visual features* and *text features.* You may want to create a chart as shown or write the features on Post-its or cards and have kids group them.

- As students "name" the features, be sure to help **standardize the language** you want them to use.

TEACHING LANGUAGE

. . . Let's review the features we have already studied: photographs, captions . . . (mention features from the *Feature/Purpose* chart). We saw that each feature is used for a specific purpose (link the purpose to the feature).

. . . Now let me show you something interesting. There are some differences in the features. For example, when we look at illustrations, we can see that they "picture" something. We call these *visual features.* (Show an example from the previous session.) Some features, like captions, are made up of words. We call these *text features.* (Show an example.) As readers, we use both visual and text features to learn more and understand more!

. . . Let's think about the features we have already studied and sort them into *visual features* and *text features.* (Examples are shown below.)

Visual Features	Text Features (Words and Letters)
photographs	bold print
illustrations	captions
drawings	titles
charts	headings
graphs	

Teach/Model

- **Begin previewing the text** with students. In this session, you will offer students an opportunity to explore the nonfiction features in a new text and gain practice in navigating them.

- Keep the *Feature/Purpose* chart on display. **Add features and purposes to the chart** if kids discover new ones.

> **Teaching Tip**
>
> If kids made a book of features in *The Primary Comprehension Toolkit* Lesson 3, refer to it. Developing a solid understanding of the reading/writing connection is important. When kids use features for authentic purposes, they gain insight about features and purposes.

. . . We will keep our *Feature/Purpose* chart handy as we look at another text and its features. We may even need to add some new features to the chart! Remember how we looked through the text and talked about all the ways the author helps us by adding visual and text features. Let's do that again.

. . . Watch me first, and then you will turn and talk with one another as you look through the text. (Be sure to identify the features as *visual features* or *text features*. Do only a few features, quickly turning the responsibility over to the students.)

. . . What were some of things you noticed as I thought aloud about the features? Did anyone notice that I used our new terms: *visual features* and *text features*?

. . . Did anyone see a new feature we should add to our chart? Wonderful! You will want to be looking for others to add.

Guide/Support Practice

TEACHING MOVES

- **Have students finish previewing** the text, looking for new features. Listen in and watch students to gain insight about their understanding of the features and the new information.

- **Ask kids to share their discoveries.** Probe to make sure they are successfully navigating the features *and* considering how the features add to their understanding.

- **Have students read the text,** paying special attention to the features.

TEACHING LANGUAGE

. . . Now it's your turn. Look through the rest of the text. See if you find any new features we should add to our chart.

. . . What did you notice? (Have students briefly talk about what they found.)

. . . Let's begin reading now, with special attention to the features. I will listen in. When I am beside you, I'd love to hear you read. When you come to a feature, name it and share what you learn from the feature. Remember, there are two types of features: visual features and text features. Okay, get started!

Wrap Up

TEACHING MOVES

- Have students **look back at the *Feature/Purpose* chart.** Add any new features or purposes to the chart.

- **Review the two types of features** and the differences between them.

TEACHING LANGUAGE

. . . Let's look back at our *Feature/Purpose* chart. Which features did you see again? Are there new features we should add? (Add any new features and discuss the purpose.)

. . . We added to our understanding today! Remember the two kinds of features? (Scaffold thinking as necessary.) Wow! I can see that you learned some important information. A feature that has just letters and words is a . . . . Ah, good! A *text* feature. What about one that pictures something? Right! A *visual* feature!

Assess and Plan

How did students' reading show growing evidence of their understanding of nonfiction features, feature types, and their purposes?
If students aren't using terms with ease, it may be helpful to reteach the session.

What additional features might students need to learn?
Consider additional texts students might read to increase the number of features they know and understand.

What additional practice could you offer students?
- Consider asking students to select a visual feature or text feature from a newspaper or magazine and label it.
- Offer students individual *Feature/Purpose* charts to use in their independent reading.
- In addition, students may begin to use features as they write nonfiction. There's no better way for students to come to an understanding of features than to use them to express or share information in writing. (See *The Primary Comprehension Toolkit* Lesson 5.)

During reading, check to make sure that students are:
- thinking about the visual features and text features as they read and leaving tracks of their thinking.
- understanding different kinds of features and the purposes they serve (how they teach us information).

Reading Conference
Monitor Comprehension

After this unit, you want to know that students are consciously making meaning, so your conference should help the student talk about both the process and the content of reading—what he or she was thinking while reading—and be aware of how nonfiction features communicate information to the reader.

1. **Invite the student to choose a passage and create a context for it.**
   - Choose a part of your book to read to me.
   - Tell me what you were thinking when you read that part.

2. **Focus in on monitoring strategies by prompting the student to talk about the text and his or her written or drawn responses.**
   - Write or draw something about what you just read. Tell me about what you wrote.
   - What did this part make you think or wonder about?
   - Does this remind you of anything? What?

3. *(If the student is reading nonfiction with visual and text features)* **Determine what the student knows about nonfiction features, their purposes, and what he or she can learn from them.**
   - What nonfiction feature(s) do you notice in your book? *(photos, labels, headings, captions)*
   - Show me a text or visual feature. What information does it give you?
   - How does this feature help you as a reader? Why do you think the author included it?

Reading Conference Recording Form: Monitor Comprehension

Name _____ Date _____

Book title _____

GOAL	EVIDENCE
The student . . .	This student . . .
1. Understands the text • Tells what the book is about and talks about what she or he was thinking while reading	
2. Is aware of what he or she thinks about the text • Writes or draws something about the text • Talks about what the text makes him or her think or wonder about • Talks about what the text reminds him or her of	
3. (If reading nonfiction with features) Knows about text and visual features and their purposes • Names text and visual features • Shares information learned from text and visual features • Explains the purpose of a feature	

©2010 by Stephanie Harvey, Anne Goudvis, and Judy Wallis. From *Comprehension Intervention: Small-Group Lessons for The Primary Comprehension Toolkit*. Portsmouth, NH: Heinemann. This page may be copied for classroom use only.

Conference Recording Form for "Monitor Comprehension," located in "Resources" section.

Language students may use to demonstrate that they are monitoring meaning

- I am thinking . . . The story makes me think about . . .
- This reminds me of . . .
- I learned . . .
- I wonder . . .

Follow-Ups

If a student has difficulty with any of the primary goals in this unit, prompts like the following may be helpful during independent work in subsequent units.

- What are you thinking?
- Does this remind you of anything? What?
- What did you learn from the nonfiction features in this text?
- Any questions?
- How can you keep track of your thinking in this book?
- You look puzzled about that part. Tell me what you are thinking right here.

Activate and Connect

The background knowledge we bring to learning colors every aspect of our understanding. Whether we are connecting, questioning, or inferring, background knowledge is the foundation of our thinking. We simply can't understand what we hear, read, or view without thinking about what we already know. To comprehend, learners must connect the new to the known. So we consider every conceivable way to build our kids' background knowledge to prepare them to learn new information. We begin by encouraging young learners to think about what they already know and care about, and then we have them explore those topics. As kids go on to read widely in nonfiction, they are bombarded with new information. In order to understand it, they need to merge their thinking with the information, stopping and reacting as they go. By making connections to what they already know, they make sense of their new learning and acquire new knowledge.

> *It is the supreme art of the teacher to awaken joy in creative expression and knowledge.* (Albert Einstein)

Companion to ...

The Primary Comprehension Toolkit
Lesson 4: Discover Your Passion

SESSION GOALS

We want students to:

- understand that nonfiction reading is "reading to learn" and nonfiction writing is "writing to teach."
- learn what a specialist is and what it means to have a passion.
- recognize that they all come to school with lots of information and that they are all specialists in something.

Learn What a "Specialist" Is

In *The Primary Comprehension Toolkit* Lesson 4, students create a specialist topic list with an eye toward writing their own teaching books. The two companion sessions supporting Lesson 4 work together to give kids more time to explore teaching texts and discover their own specialist passions. In this first session, students deepen their understanding of the reading/writing connection and what it means to be a specialist.

TEXT MATTERS

To help kids deepen the reading/writing connection, we show them what nonfiction is: reading to learn and writing to teach. To make the point, gather nonfiction books, magazines, and articles on a range of topics that will engage kids through their own interests and curiosity. Motivation to read is always fueled by interest. Consider what you know about your students' interests as you select the texts you will share.

Select books with interesting covers, such as *Honey in a Hive* by Anne Rockwell and *Bread, Bread, Bread* by Ann Morris; nonfiction magazines, such as *National Geographic Kids*, *Ranger Rick*, and *Click*; and engaging short texts, such as "Totem Poles, Family Stories" and "We Take Care of Our Pet" from *Keep Reading*.

CONSIDERATIONS FOR PLANNING

Make room to spread out the texts so kids can see the covers. This session capitalizes on students' interests and offers them authentic purposes to make connections to their background experience as they make new discoveries about their passions.

The goal is to show kids what it means to be a "specialist." By explaining that specialists know and care a lot about one topic, we offer kids real-life purposes and audiences for their knowledge. Our modeling in this session prepares students to develop a list of specialist topics that can spill over into writing.

Build Background, Word and Concept Knowledge

- **Engage kids through a display of books and magazines.** Because of the small-group setting, kids will be able to see the covers with ease. Select one or two especially interesting covers to explore with the kids.

- During the book and magazine browsing, be sure to note the nonfiction features students have been discussing. **Use the terms** *visual features* **and** *text features.*

- As you build further background about non-fiction, help kids **develop the concept that a "specialist" teaches through writing** non-fiction books and articles.

- As you explore the examples, help kids develop the concept of being a specialist—**a specialist knows a lot about something and cares a lot about it.**

- Engage kids as you look at the different books and magazines by having them predict the content. **Page through some of the books** to see what is inside.

. . . We are going to learn something very important today! I thought of you and all the things you are interested in. Then I gathered lots of wonderful books and magazines to share with you. Look at this one . . . and this one. So interesting! As we look at all these texts written by people who were connecting to their own interests, I want us to think about *why* we read nonfiction and *why* authors write it. Here are the reasons: we read nonfiction to get information, and authors write nonfiction to give us information.

. . . For example, I am really interested in (gardening), so I enjoy finding a new book or magazine article that teaches me new things. I am a specialist because I know about and am always eager to learn more about (gardening). (Teachers should talk about their own interests here as a model.)

. . . Let's think about that word *specialist* for a minute. Why do you think someone would write a whole book on (bees)? Turn and talk about that.

. . . Ideas? Right! They are really, really interested in (bees), they know a lot about (bees), and they want to share what they know. They are specialists!

. . . Here is another interesting thing! Specialists use words that connect to their interests. So when I speak about (gardening), I use words related to that topic. It is almost as though I have another whole language—the language of (gardening). I have heard some of you use words I didn't know about (dinosaurs) because you are specialists, too!

. . . Today we will explore some of these books and magazines and also talk about important topics you're interested in—you are specialists, too.

Teach/Model

- Have kids look at more examples and **say what kind of specialist they think each author is.**

- **Create an anchor chart** to reinforce the term and concept of *specialists*.

- Model how to **create a "Specialist Topic List"** so kids understand the thinking that goes into its creation.

> **Teaching Tip**
>
> The more opportunities kids have to use a new word that stands for a concept, the deeper their understanding goes. Be sure to use the word *specialist* and anchor it to the meaning and concept.

. . . All these great teaching books and magazines are written by people who are specialists in something they are passionate about. Look at this one. What do you think this person is interested in? What kind of specialist is this author?

. . . Let's make a chart. I will write *Specialists* on it and list what they do. Let's look at what I am writing (think aloud as you add to the chart).

. . . Now, I am going to write some ideas to explore—some topics I am interested in—things I like to think about *and* maybe even want to teach others. (Add your own interests here. For young children, consider drawing illustrations as you write so they connect the words to the pictures.)

Specialists:

- Know a lot about something
- Care a lot about something that is interesting to them
- Want to share and teach others

Specialist Topic List

Guide/Support Practice

- Have kids **reread the chart.** The practice part of this session is a transition between what the teacher did and what kids will do in the next session. The practice involves thinking about the concept of being a specialist and the process of creating a specialist list.

- Tell kids that next time they will make their own specialist topic list. **Invite them to start thinking** about how they can get started.

. . . Let's reread the chart and my topic list.

. . . Now here is *your* job! When we meet again, I am going to ask you to do the same thing I did— make a "specialist list." So, you should be thinking hard about what your list will include.

. . . Let's think of some things you could do to get started. Turn and talk for a minute about that.

. . . Suggestions? Good one! You could look in the basket of nonfiction books I have gathered for topics you know a lot about, like . . . . (Generate as many suggestions as possible.)

Wrap Up

- **Reread your topic list** with kids.

- **Ask students to share their ideas.** Probe for more topics if kids generate only one or two. Here are some probes:
  - What do you like to read about or talk about at home?
  - What do you like to watch on TV? (Mention educational channels you know kids watch.)
  - When you draw, what kinds of things do you like to draw?
  - Do you have any collections at home?

. . . Let's look back at my list and read it together.

. . . Your job is to think of topics you could list. Who has an idea or ideas already? (Allow kids to share a few.)

. . . Great! I can hardly wait for the next time we meet! Don't forget what your job is—be thinking hard about topics you could list.

ASSESS AND PLAN

What did you notice about students' engagement with the texts you gathered?

If students were not eagerly engaged, you may want to spend a bit more time delving into a few books you know would interest the group members.

Did students seem ready to identify topics?

Consider taking time to talk with students individually before they create their lists. Use the probing questions to help scaffold thinking. You might team up with the media specialist or schedule time in the library to help students generate interest in a topic they already know about. But remember, this session and the following one are all about sharing what kids *already know and care about*.

Choose a Topic for a Teaching Book

Writing is thinking on paper.
(William Zinsser)

This session picks up where the previous session leaves off. Students review the concept of a specialist, write their specialist topic list, and choose a topic for their teaching book. Students will plan and write their books in Sessions 5a and 5b.

Companion to . . .

The Primary Comprehension Toolkit
Lesson 4: Discover Your Passion

TEXT MATTERS

Have the books and magazines from the previous session available so you can reinforce the concept that authors are specialists and that we write to teach and read to learn. Be enthusiastic about your own interests. Kids will catch your passion for learning.

CONSIDERATIONS FOR PLANNING

This session connects to the previous one and extends the invitation to kids to *be* a specialist. By supporting students as they uncover and share their own passions, we help them understand the social nature of literacy. When we are interested in a topic, we are eager to share what we know about it with others.

Have the *Specialists* anchor chart and your own topic list available.

SESSION GOALS

We want students to:

- review what a specialist is and what it means to have a passion.
- recognize that they all come to school with lots of information and that they are all specialists in something.
- create a list of specialist topics that they know a lot about, care about, and could teach someone about.

Build Background, Word and Concept Knowledge

TEACHING MOVES

- **Briefly review** the books and magazines, building enthusiasm for students' identification of their own interests.

- **Remind kids about specialists:** A specialist is someone who knows a lot about something and cares a lot about it. Specialists want to teach others what they know.

- Help students see that **authors have a specialized language or vocabulary** that goes with their topics. The concept of a "network of words" builds vocabulary and helps kids see how words relate to topics and ideas.

TEACHING LANGUAGE

. . . Let's think again about the word *specialist*. Remember we talked about how all these authors are specialists. They wanted to teach us about something in which they are very interested. Turn and talk about what you notice about the topics these authors write about.

. . . Share some of the topics you notice as you look through the books and magazines.

. . . Authors have a whole "specialized" language they use to teach us about their topics. (Select a topic and build a network of words around the topic. Example: *bees: hive, comb, honey, buzz, queen*)

Teach/Model

TEACHING MOVES

- **Review the** *Specialists* **anchor chart** and your topic list so kids recall the thinking that went into their creation. You may use a pointer or have the students use one as they read from the *Specialists* chart.

- **Rethink aloud** your own collection of topics to prepare students to create their own.

TEACHING LANGUAGE

. . . Today you'll have your turn to create a "Specialist Topic List" just like I did last time!

. . . Let's look back at the chart we made about what a specialist is. Turn and talk with your neighbor about what you see. What are the important ideas here? (Have kids read from the chart.)

. . . I want to share my list with you again, too. Let's look at it. Remember, I put this topic here because . . . Oh, and this one is here because I am so fascinated by . . .

. . . I'm going to ask you now to make your own lists. I know you have been thinking and thinking about what you'll write.

Guide/Support Practice

- Ask kids to quickly **turn and talk about their specialties.** Offering kids an oral rehearsal is a great way to help them get started and a good way to informally assess and determine who will need more support.

- **Have students make their list.** You can give them paper to use, or copy the form provided on page 65 in *The Primary Comprehension Toolkit Strategy Book 2: Activate and Connect.*

- **Support students as they write,** nudging where there is hesitation. Make sure the books and magazines are handy, and refer to the topics to help students find their own passions.

. . . Quickly, turn and talk about your specialties. You are all specialists about something!

. . . I'm going to give each of you paper to make your own lists. Here's what you'll do. Write the word *Topics* at the top of the page. Then make three "bullets." Remember, when we talked about text features, we said that a bullet signals a new idea.

Topics

-
-
-

. . . As you think of things you are passionate about, add them to your list right beside a bullet. You may even need *more* bullets!

. . . Let's see what you have written. Turn and talk about your lists of the topics you'd like to teach another person about.

. . . Anyone find something new to add after chatting?

. . . Right this minute, think of a topic that is tugging at you—one you just find so exciting and want to share. Circle that topic because you will soon have a chance to capture your own thinking in writing.

Wrap Up

TEACHING MOVES

- Encourage students to **keep thinking about their topic** of choice. One important part of a writer's life is looking everywhere for good ideas to include. Our work is helping kids "live" like readers and writers!

TEACHING LANGUAGE

. . . Great thinking today! This was really interesting, but the best part comes next, when you will write your very own teaching book. When we write, we share our knowledge with others, and *we* learn, too!

. . . Be thinking about your topic. You may want to jot some notes to track your thinking. Your thinking and your notes will help you author your own teaching book.

ASSESS AND PLAN

What did you notice about students' thinking as they created their lists? What additional support might some students need from you?

If students have difficulty identifying their interests, create time to confer with them individually. Sometimes only one or two minutes can make a huge difference. Don Graves talked about "nudge paper." If, as a reluctant student talks, you hear a good idea, name it for the student and write it on a small piece of paper or a Post-it. This "nudge paper," left with the student, is tangible evidence of the student's good thinking. You may also suggest more book browsing.

Plan a Teaching Book

"Rehearsal refers to the preparation for composing and can take the form of daydreaming, sketching, doodling, making lists of words, outlining . . . ."
(Graves, 2003)

Companion to . . .

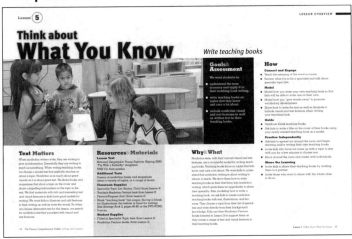

The Primary Comprehension Toolkit
Lesson 5: Think about What You Know

In *The Primary Comprehension Toolkit* Lesson 5, students write directly from their background knowledge to author a teaching book. The two companion sessions for Lesson 5 offer students an alternate approach for writing a teaching book. In this first session, kids use Post-its to jot down ideas and plan their pages.

TEXT MATTERS

The same books, magazines, and articles you used as resources in previous sessions will continue to serve an important role as models for students' writing. Kids can refer to them for examples of visual and text features, organization, accuracy, and so on.

CONSIDERATIONS FOR PLANNING

This session draws from the students' experiences over the past few sessions. Now that students have identified a topic and studied how nonfiction authors use visual and text features, they apply that learning in writing their own teaching books.

We want students to create texts with a range of visual and text features and to draw from their background knowledge, using all they know to write about their topic.

Have the *Specialists* anchor chart and the *Feature/Purpose* chart available.

Prepare "blank books" of 4–8 pages, depending on the length of books you expect the students to write. For masters, see *The Primary Comprehension Toolkit Strategy Book 2: Activate and Connect*, pages 66–68. Blank paper that has been stapled works equally well. For older students, you may want to fold the paper in half and staple. Younger students will likely need a whole sheet for each page.

Students will need the topic lists they created in Session 4b.

Students will need Post-its.

SESSION GOALS

We want students to:

- understand the term *accuracy* and apply it to their teaching book writing.

- prepare to write teaching books.

- review nonfiction visual and text features to prepare to write their own books.

Build Background, Word and Concept Knowledge

- **Reinforce the idea of a specialist.** Use the *Specialists* anchor chart as shared reading so kids connect the concepts of being a specialist, writing teaching books, being accurate, and using visual and text features to help communicate a message and increase comprehension.

- Take time to **teach the concept of** *accuracy* by offering examples. Because nonfiction authors write to teach—to share information—accuracy is critical. Make sure kids understand the importance of accuracy.

Teaching Tip

As kids plan and write their books, help them consider what nonfiction writers do. Authors think about their topic, audience, purpose, and form (organization); where to find or check information; and how other authors have organized their books.

. . . Remember when we looked through this text? The writer taught us a great deal about _____. This author is a specialist. The author knows so much about _____, and by reading the text, we learn!

. . . You have identified your own specialties—topics you know lots about!

. . . One very, very important thing we haven't yet talked about is a nonfiction writer's responsibility to be accurate! This is so important. *Accurate* means that what you say is true. For example, I can't describe a frog as the size of a house because that wouldn't be accurate! When we write our own books, we must be careful to be sure we are teaching our reader only correct, or accurate, information.

. . . Turn and talk with your neighbor about being accurate. What does it mean? I bet you can use an example!

Teach/Model

- **Review your topic list** so kids recall the thinking that went into its creation. You may use a pointer or have the students use one as they reread from the *Specialists* anchor chart.

- Model how you **choose a topic** from your list.

- **Reinforce the need to be *accurate*** as you think about what you will write. Give a student the word *accurate* on a Post-it. Modeling how you "give words away" helps kids make the connection that their own words are gifts to others, particularly in teaching books.

- Model how you **plan your teaching book, using Post-its** to record and arrange your ideas. Make your thinking and planning visible to students. The more modeling you do, the more successful students will be on their first attempts.

- **Thinking aloud is essential.** Kids must see your composing process. It will serve as a powerful model of what they will do in their own writing.

. . . Remember, my specialist topic list includes three topics—things I am very interested in.

. . . After thinking about these three topics, I've decided to write a teaching book about _____. I selected that topic because I am really interested in it, and I would like others to know more about it. I will make sure when I write that all my information is very accurate! What does that mean? Turn and talk!

. . . I am going to write the word *accurate* on a Post-it and give it away to _____. If anyone wonders about the meaning of the word *accurate*, check in with _____.

. . . Now let me show you how I start to write my book. I'm going to think about important ideas, or information, that I want to include. I need to think of an idea for each page. I will put each idea on a Post-it. I think I need to teach about . . . (Identify and write two or three ideas you think are important for your topic. Write each on a separate Post-it.)

. . . Now I need to think about the best order for my ideas—the order that will make the most sense to my reader, the person I will teach! I think I need to write about . . . first. (Put numbers on the Post-its so kids see how they will plan their own books. As you number, stick each Post-it on a page of your blank book.)

. . . I have a plan now. Let's get started making your plans!

Guide/Support Practice

- Have students **write information about their topic,** using Post-its. Offer support as needed. Help students think of the ideas that will be the focus of each page. If students have been taught the concept of main idea and details, that language might be helpful here.

- Have students **plan their books** by arranging their Post-its on the pages.

. . . Turn your topic lists over and put the topic you want to write about at the top of the page.

. . . Here are Post-its for everyone. Now, just as I did, jot down your information, or smaller ideas, one to a Post-it. Stick the Post-its under your topic. (Offer support as necessary.)

. . . Once you have your smaller ideas written on the Post-its, see how you want to arrange them. Put 1, 2, 3, . . . on them. Once you are happy with the order, put one at the very bottom of each page of your blank book. That will help you as you begin to write.

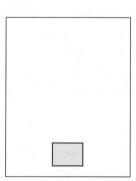

Wrap Up

- Encourage students to **keep thinking about their ideas.**

. . . You worked really hard today. Next time we meet, we will start writing. I will show you how I write my book first.

. . . Be thinking about what you want to say on each page of your teaching book. You may want to jot some notes to track your thinking. Your thinking and notes will help you write your book.

ASSESS AND PLAN

Do some students need extra support?

If students haven't been able to do their planning, consider using shared or interactive writing as an alternate approach. Plan a teaching book together.

As teachers, you are able to "light the fire." What could be better than that? (Swan, 2003)

Write a Teaching Book

This session picks up where the previous session leaves off. Students use their Post-it notes to write their teaching books.

Companion to . . .

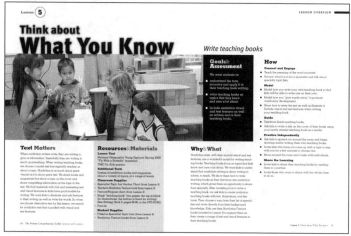

The Primary Comprehension Toolkit
Lesson 5: Think about What You Know

SESSION GOALS

We want students to:

- understand the term *accuracy* and apply it to their teaching book writing.

- write teaching books on topics that they know and care a lot about.

- include nonfiction visual and text features as well as written text in their teaching books.

TEXT MATTERS

Continue to have the same books, magazines, and articles available. They will continue to play an important role as models, especially for visual and text features.

CONSIDERATIONS FOR PLANNING

This session connects to the previous three and draws on students' experiences in identifying and planning a topic. During this session, they will write their teaching books.

Keep reinforcing how visual and text features can help readers in learning about each child's topic. Kids will use visual and text features to teach information as they write their books.

Continue to have the *Specialists* anchor chart and the *Feature/Purpose* chart visible. Students will refer to them in writing their books.

Students will need their blank books with Post-its in them from the previous session.

Build Background, Word and Concept Knowledge

TEACHING MOVES

- **Engage kids in a review** of what they did in the previous sessions.

- **Focus kids on using visual and text features** to help communicate their message.

- **Invite kids to share** their topics and one of their Post-it notes.

- **Focus students on being accurate** as they write. Take time, if necessary, to reteach the concept of accuracy in nonfiction writing.

TEACHING LANGUAGE

. . . Let's review what we have done so far. Who can get us started?

. . . Right! We studied nonfiction books and saw how the authors are specialists. And we noticed how visual and text features really help in teaching books. (Continue to help students connect with the background knowledge about nonfiction writing that they have built over the past few sessions.)

. . . You have done some planning for your own teaching books. You are going to continue those today, writing and illustrating them as you go.

. . . Who wants to share your topic and one of your Post-it notes?

. . . Great! Thanks for sharing. Being accurate is really important. How can we be sure we are accurate? Turn and talk about that.

Teach/Model

■ Model how you **begin writing your book.** Make your thinking and planning visible to students. The more modeling you do, the more successful students will be on their first attempts.

■ Show students how you **expand an idea into several sentences.**

■ **Think aloud about visual or text features** that might be helpful to the reader.

. . . Now let me show you how I write my book. I am going to illustrate and add text features as I go.

. . . I need to make a cover first. See how I write the title. I am going to call my book _____. Now I will write my name: by _____. An illustration that would help my readers predict my topic and feel eager to read is . . .

. . . On this page I put a Post-it with one idea on it. My idea is _____. I am going to write some information about it. I'll write . . . (Show how you expand that idea into several sentences.) I think it would help the reader if I added a labeled drawing here to show . . . Notice how I am teaching accurate information about _____.

. . . I am going to continue for another page. Then it will be your turn to write your own books. (Model how you write information about the next idea, adding visual or text features.)

Guide/Support Practice

- **Have kids write their teaching books,** expanding on the ideas they wrote on their Post-its, developing the information into sentences, and adding visual and text features.

- Move from student to student to **offer support as needed.** Help students understand the smaller ideas that will be the focus of each page.

. . . Now it's your turn!

. . . I am going to be right here to help you as you write. But remember, *you* are the specialist about your topic!

Wrap Up

- **Invite kids to share** what they have done so far.

- Encourage students to **keep thinking about their ideas.**

- Remind them to **check their accuracy.**

. . . Let's see what you've done. Turn and share with a partner.

. . . Who has something they want everyone to see?

. . . I can hardly wait to read the great books you are writing! Remember, it's important to be sure you are accurate. One way to do that is to look in books about your very same topic to check for accuracy. When you're ready, you can do that.

ASSESS AND PLAN

Do some students need extra time or support?

Arrange time to confer with those students who need extra support. If they continue to struggle, co-author the writing with them. Most students will then be able to add the illustrations and other features.

Check to be sure that students:

- have used features, such as illustrations, labels, diagrams, and captions, to teach about their topic. There's no better way to demonstrate understanding than by writing and drawing features themselves.

Good readers know how to 'wake up' and use the information they have about a topic in order to help them understand what they are reading. (Tovani, 2000)

Make Text-to-Self Connections

The Primary Comprehension Toolkit Lesson 6 engages students in making personal connections with a realistic-fiction read-aloud. The two companion sessions for Lesson 6 offer students additional support for making connections to realistic fiction. In this session, students focus on listening to the inner voice and making text-to-self connections. In the next session, they add text-to-text connections.

Companion to . . .

The Primary Comprehension Toolkit
Lesson 6: Make Connections

TEXT MATTERS

For this session on listening to the inner voice, select a text that the kids can connect to easily. Many realistic-fiction stories for young readers portray situations kids frequently experience. Books by Kevin Henkes, Tomie de Paola, Aliki, and Ezra Jack Keats are terrific for making text-to-self connections.

Articles such as "Having a Ball Playing Soccer" and "A Ladybug's Life" in *Keep Reading* also invite kids to make text-to-self connections.

CONSIDERATIONS FOR PLANNING

All readers are influenced by their background knowledge and experience. Proficient readers automatically make connections to their personal experiences. If we listen to the inner voice, we often hear "This reminds me of . . ." or "I remember when . . . ." Because connecting to our own experience enriches reading, we teach students to make personal connections and use them to deepen their understanding of a text.

However, it is easy to allow personal experiences to lead us off on tangents rather than toward meaning. This session is designed to ensure kids use their background knowledge and personal experiences to further their understanding of a text.

Students will need Post-its.

SESSION GOALS

We want students to:

- understand what it means to make a connection to the text.
- understand that their personal experience is important to understanding what they read and learn.
- learn to listen to their inner voice to make sense of text.

Build Background, Word and Concept Knowledge

- This session focuses on building an awareness of the inner voice and using that inside-the-head conversation to **make meaningful text-to-self connections.**

- **Explain what you mean by the _inner voice_,** so that students understand and begin to listen for it.

. . . Today we are going to learn something so exciting! Have you ever overheard someone say something that they were really just saying to themselves? I sometimes talk to myself when I am trying to figure something out or when I see something interesting or confusing. For example, the other day I saw a man getting out of his car during a storm. He was trying to get his umbrella to stay up. I immediately said to myself, "I had that happen once and I got all wet! I was so mad." (Substitute your own authentic example.)

. . . I could easily connect with what was happening to the man because I had experienced something similar. Watching him helped me understand how the man must be feeling right then.

. . . Good readers do that kind of thing all the time. They notice things the author has included in the story and it reminds them of something. It is the _inner voice_ that signals us and says, "Wow, here is something I know about!"

Teach/Model

- **Introduce the text** and let kids hear your inner voice as you think about the cover and/or title. Explicit modeling is critical here.

- Ask kids to **share what their inner voice is saying** about the cover/title. If you hear kids sharing things that are off-target, continue to think aloud and model your own inner conversation.

- **Introduce the term** *text-to-self connection* and explain how readers naturally think about what they already know as they are reading.

- Model how you **make and record a text-to-self connection** to the cover/title. Think aloud as you write and/or draw it on a Post-it and code it with *T-S* for *text-to-self connection*.

- **Preview unfamiliar vocabulary** or concepts using the context of the story to discuss them.

. . . Today we are going to learn about the inner voice and how it can help us understand what we read. Let me show you how it works. I brought a terrific book for us to read (share the title). When I look at the cover, I hear my inner voice saying, "Oh, wow . . ." (connect to the title and cover illustration).

. . . Good readers "talk" to and with their texts. They think about what they are reading all the time. I'll bet some of you are hearing your own inner voices. Turn and talk about what you are hearing and thinking about the cover.

. . . Who wants to share what your inner voice is saying?

. . . I heard many of you talking about connecting to something that happened in your own life. When we make that kind of connection, we call it a *text-to-self* connection and we code it like this: *T-S*.

. . . I have a text-to-self connection to the cover. I remember a time when . . . (connect your own experience to the cover). I am going to record my connection like this. (Write and/or draw your thinking on a Post-it and code it *T-S*.)

```
┌─────────────────────┐
│  T–S                │
│                     │
│  I was _____.      │
│                     │
└─────────────────────┘
```

. . . Before we read, there are some words we need to talk about. Here's one . . .

. . . Now I am going to start reading. I'll show you how I listen to my inner conversation and record it. (Continue for only another page or two.)

Guide/Support Practice

TEACHING MOVES

- **Have kids read, recording their connections** on Post-its. Use guided practice time to offer individual support to the students who are most likely to struggle without additional scaffolding. They may need side-by-side support.

- **Move about the group,** listening in to students' reading and thinking. Nudge them if they don't naturally share their thinking. Ask, "What is your inner voice saying as you read the part right here?"

- Remind kids to **code *T-S* connections.**

- **If the text is too long to finish,** stop kids after they have read enough to record a few connections. You can continue with the same text in the next session.

TEACHING LANGUAGE

. . . Now it is your turn to read on. I'll give each of you some Post-its. Stop and record when your inner voice says, "This reminds me of my . . . I remember when I . . . ."

. . . Remember, you are connecting what's happening in the book to your own experiences. You can write *T-S* on the Post-it to show that it is a text-to-self connection.

. . . I will be coming by to listen in on your reading and your inner "thinking" voice, too, when you hear it talking to you.

Wrap Up

TEACHING MOVES

- **Ask kids to share** one or two of their Post-its.

- **Have kids review** what they learned about the inner voice and text-to-self connections.

TEACHING LANGUAGE

. . . I heard lots of good thinking as I listened in on your reading. (Ask one or two kids to share what their inner voice said and what they recorded.)

. . . So let's think about what we did today. We learned that all of us have a voice inside our heads that helps us notice when we make a connection to our own experiences.

. . . Turn and talk about how those connections are helpful. Remember what we called them? Right, *text-to-self* connections!

ASSESS AND PLAN

What did you notice about students' thinking as you listened to them read?

If students rarely paused and just kept reading, they likely aren't listening to the voice in their head. You may want to help them decide where to stop and listen for the voice in their head by reading part of the text to them. Sometimes slowing a reader down increases comprehension because they are stopping to think about their reading.

What did students write or draw on their Post-its? Did they make meaningful connections?

Look through students' Post-its and assess their understanding. If children's responses are vague or are not substantive connections linking their experiences with the characters or events of the text, confer with readers to offer extra support.

We tend to respond and talk back to nonfiction texts more than to other texts, and it is helpful to encourage children to do this. (Calkins, 2001)

Make Text-to-Text Connections

This session builds on the previous one. This time, students focus on making text-to-text connections.

Companion to . . .

The Primary Comprehension Toolkit
Lesson 6: Make Connections

TEXT MATTERS

If students did not complete the text from the previous session, continue in the same text. If they completed it, you can have them reread it, as the practice of repeated readings promotes both comprehension and fluency. Or select another text that will encourage kids to make both text-to-self and text-to-text connections.

Short articles such as "The Horse Close Up" and "Rock Secrets" in *Toolkit Texts: Grades 2–3* have topics familiar to most students. These allow kids to make text-to-text as well as text-to-self connections.

CONSIDERATIONS FOR PLANNING

This session continues the focus on listening to the inner voice. In addition to listening for *text-to-self* connections, students learn to make *text-to-text* connections: connections between the text they are reading and other "texts," including books, movies, even TV shows. Making text-to-text connections increases students' comprehension and potential for seeing patterns across texts. It is a strategy they will build upon throughout the years.

Be prepared to create a *My Connection/How It Helps Me Understand* chart with the students. For a form you can copy for kids' independent reading, see *The Primary Comprehension Toolkit Strategy Book 2: Activate and Connect*, pages 70–72.

Students will need Post-its.

SESSION GOALS

We want students to:

- understand what it means to make a connection to the text.
- understand that their personal experience is important to understanding what they read and learn.
- learn to listen to their inner voice to make sense of text.

Build Background, Word and Concept Knowledge

- **Review what kids know** about the inner voice, using examples from the previous session. Using authentic student examples will help readers connect to their experiences and build upon them.

- **Make a chart** with the headings *My Connection/ How It Helps Me Understand*. Tell kids that as you model reading and listening to your inner voice, you will record your connections and how they help you understand the text. "How it helps me understand" will, of course, depend on the text you are reading with the kids.

- **If you are using a new text,** show the cover and/or title and invite students to share their initial connections. Preview pertinent vocabulary or ideas so kids can focus on making connections as they read.

. . . Remember how we talked about listening to our inner voice? Well, today we will have more opportunities to do that. I recall that _____ remembered a time when he . . . , and he connected that to the story when . . .

. . . Does anyone remember what we called that kind of connection? Right! It is a *text-to-self* connection! Turn and talk for a moment about the connections we made when we were last reading.

. . . Great! Remember, it is the inner voice that signals us and says, "Here is something I can connect to!"

. . . To help us, I am going to make a chart. When I make a connection, I am going to record it in the chart. Then I am going to jot down how it helps me better understand the story (or text).

My Connection	How It Helps Me Understand

. . . (If using a new text, preview it with kids.) Let's look at the text we're going to read. What connections are you making already? There are a few words you'll need to know . . .

Teach/Model

- **Explain** *text-to-text connections* and how readers naturally think about other books, movies, and television shows.

- Begin to read and **use both kinds of connections.** Stop from time to time to share how both are connections and draw from our knowledge and past experiences. The difference is one connects to our personal experiences and the other reminds us of our reading life.

- Continued modeling is critical here. Be sure to **let kids turn and talk.** Listen in so you know what they hear their inner voice saying.

- Ask kids to share what they hear their inner voice saying. **Record a few of their connections** on the chart.

- As you read on, show kids how to **record and code a connection on a Post-it.**

> **Teaching Tip**
> Readers can find themselves distracted by a powerful memory or personal connection. Watch for opportunities to help kids see the difference between connections that create understanding and those that interfere with thinking.

. . . Today we're going to continue listening to the inner voice and making text-to-self connections. And we're going to learn about one *more* kind of connection: *text-to-text.*

. . . Sometimes you read a book or see a movie and you say, "Wow, that really reminds me of another book or movie." That is a *text-to-text connection.* The more books we read, the more text-to-text connections we make!

. . . I'll show you how this works. (Read a portion of the text. When you find a place to make a text-to-text connection, record it on the chart. If you read or reread a portion where you have a text-to-self connection, point that out to students and note it on the chart.)

. . . Some of you are hearing your own inner voices. Turn and talk about what you are hearing and thinking. Remember, you can make either a text-to-self or a text-to-text connection.

. . . Anyone want to share what your inner voice is saying? (Add students' connections to the chart.)

. . . I'll continue reading. Ah, here is a place I have a text-to-text connection. When . . . happened, it reminded me of . . . in another book. I am going to write my connection on a Post-it. And here is the code I will use: *T-T.* (Record on the Post-it.)

Guide/Support Practice

TEACHING MOVES

- **Have kids read,** listening to their inner voice and recording and coding connections on their Post-its.

- Provide side-by-side coaching and reteaching as necessary to help students. **Probe with questions** that kids can ask themselves to gain meaning.

TEACHING LANGUAGE

. . . Now it's your turn to read on. I will give you each more Post-its. Stop and record when your inner voice says, "This reminds me of something that happened to me" or "This reminds me of what happened in another story _____, when _____."

. . . I will be coming by to listen in on your reading and your inner "thinking" voice, too, when you hear it talking to you. Remember to record your connections on Post-its, and write *T-S* and *T-T* to code them.

Wrap Up

TEACHING MOVES

- **Have kids share** a few Post-its. Articulate and reinforce the kinds of connections students are making.

- **Have students look back at the chart.** Discuss how their connections helped them understand the story/text. You may want to add a few examples to the chart.

- **Give students copies of the chart** to use as they read in their independent books. You can copy the form on pages 70–72 in *The Primary Toolkit Strategy Book 2: Activate and Connect.* Or have kids make their own charts.

- Students' charts will provide **excellent formative assessments** to use in instructional planning.

TEACHING LANGUAGE

. . . I heard lots of good thinking as I listened in on your reading. Who would like to share something your inner voice said? (Ask one or two students to share what their inner voice said and what they recorded.)

. . . Let's think about what we did today. We used the voice inside our heads to help us notice when we make a connection to our own experiences and also to another text. Let's look back at our chart to see how our connections helped us understand the story. (Review these as a group. You may want to add some examples.)

. . . I am going to give each of you a small chart like the chart we made together. As you read in your independent books, use the chart to record your connections. In the next few days, I want you to bring those to share!

Assess and Plan

What did you notice about students' thinking as you listened to them read?
Consider the kinds of connections students were making. If connections were superficial or didn't support comprehension, consider extra support.

What kinds of connections came most easily for students?
Consider which kinds of connections students made most often. Plan to use books in read-aloud that will give additional opportunities for connections.

Do students seem to need more practice?
Use the small, student charts during whole group read-aloud. This will give students more opportunities to use their new learning!

> *Nothing colors our thinking more than what we bring to it.* (Harvey and Goudvis, 2007)

Companion to ...

The Primary Comprehension Toolkit
Lesson 7: Merge Thinking with New Learning

Identify New Information

The Primary Comprehension Toolkit Lesson 7 engages students in thinking about and reacting to information during a class read-aloud. The two companion sessions for Lesson 7 offer students more time and support for merging their thinking with new learning. In this first session, students review the concepts *background knowledge* and *facts* and focus on identifying new information as they read.

Text Matters

Select a text that will allow kids to draw on their background knowledge and learn new facts as they read. Texts that include powerful images will engage kids in thinking about new information.

Short articles such as "Clouds" in *Toolkit Texts: Grades 2–3* and "Community Helpers" in *Keep Reading* have enough information to allow kids to identify new learning.

Students also need to read books they can sink their teeth into. *What's Out There: A Book about Space* by Lynn Wilson and *Frogs* by Gail Gibbons are good choices for guided or independent reading.

Considerations for Planning

In this session, the focus is on having an inner conversation with non-fiction. We listen to the voice in our heads to learn new information. While this comes naturally to proficient readers, we need to model the process for kids as they are learning. As students note new facts and ideas, they need to merge or combine their own knowledge with new information. Listening to their inner voice helps them notice and name new learning with phrases like, "Wow, that's interesting! I never knew that . . ." By listening to their inner voice, kids slow reading down so they can merge their thinking with new learning.

Students will need Post-its.

Session Goals

We want students to:

- listen to the voice in their head that signals new learning.
- understand the term *background knowledge (BK)*.
- stop, think, and react to new information.
- mark Post-its with *L* (for *learn*) when they learn something new.

Build Background, Word and Concept Knowledge

- **Remind kids that we read nonfiction to learn.** We listen for the inner voice that signals new learning and merge the new learning with what we already know.

- **Introduce the term *background knowledge* (BK).** Explain that the inner voice signals that we just read or saw something we didn't know. The inner voice causes us to stop and think about the new information—the *facts*.

- **Review the term *facts*.** Since nonfiction has lots of facts, connect the meaning of the word *fact* to the discussion students had earlier about accuracy. When something is accurate, it is factual.

. . . Remember when we talked about our teaching books? We looked at books written by specialists, and then we created our own books about something we already knew a lot about. But, here's the thing—we can always learn something more!

. . . When we *already* know something, we call it *background knowledge*, or *BK* for short. We always think about our background knowledge, or what we already know, when we learn something new. It is like adding links on a chain. We have a chain of knowledge, and when we learn something new, we add more links to it.

. . . Today we are going to see how our inner voice signals us that we are meeting new information. As we learn new information, we build on what we already know.

. . . In our reading, we are going to be learning lots of new information. We will learn *facts*. Who can tell me what facts are? Right! Facts are ideas that are true and accurate and correct. Remember, when we wrote our teaching books, we talked about how important it is to be accurate.

Teach/Model

- **Introduce the text and topic.** Invite kids to look at the cover/title and share what they notice and what they already know. Scan the text and model how you stop and think when you notice new information.

- **Start a chart** of what the inner voice says when it recognizes new information. Focus on language "stems" that signal new information, something learned. In the next session, you will add to the chart.

> **My Inner Voice Says**
>
> Wow! This is cool!
>
> Amazing!
>
> A fact I didn't know
>
> Interesting!

- **Begin to read and model** how you listen to the inner voice and notice new information. Write or draw the information on Post-its and code them with an *L*. Be sure to model explicitly. Model how you use charts, illustrations, and other visual and text features. Think aloud about what you do—how you integrate the additional information into your thinking and reading.

- Before kids read on their own, **preview pertinent vocabulary** or concepts that may be new to them. Demonstrate how you use your background knowledge and the context to make sense of these words.

. . . I found a great book titled . . . I know many of you are really interested in _____ (topic). In addition to the great things this book can teach us, the illustrations and photographs are terrific!

. . . Look at the cover, and turn and talk about what you notice. Does the cover make you think of anything you already know?

. . . I am going to flip through the first pages of the book. Let's look for things we already know about _____. What we know will help us learn.

. . . I see lots of information—some facts I don't know. I am going to show you how I stop and think about what I know and how I notice new information. As I am reading, the voice inside my head slows me down and says, "This is interesting! I never knew this!" (Be sure to help kids notice that some information is in visual and text features.)

. . . Let's start a chart of some of the things our inner voices say. We'll title it *My Inner Voice Says.* What are some things you say when you find new information? (Let students brainstorm a range of words and phrases.)

. . . I'll read a bit and show you what I do when I find information that is new to me. I draw or jot it down on a Post-it. (Model how you read and write or draw on a Post-it.) I'll code this Post-it with an *L* for *learned.*

. . . Let's read a bit more to see what else we can find. (Model and have kids turn and talk until you see they are ready to try it themselves.)

. . . Let's talk about some words you need to know . . .

Guide/Support Practice

- **Have students read,** listening to their inner voice and recording new information on Post-its. Remind them to code new learning with an *L*.

- **Move about the group to listen in** to kids' reading and thinking. Nudge them if they don't naturally share their thinking. Ask, "Have you discovered anything you didn't know?"

- **If the text is too long to finish,** tell kids where to stop reading. You can continue with the same text for the next session.

. . . Now it is your turn to read on. I will give each of you some Post-its. Stop and record when your inner voice says, "Wow!" or "I never knew . . ." After you write or draw, code with an *L* to show your new learning.

. . . I will be coming by to listen in on your reading and thinking.

Wrap Up

- **Ask students to share** one or two of their Post-its.

- **Revisit the chart** to add any additional words or phrases kids heard their inner voices saying.

. . . I heard lots of good thinking and learning as I listened in on your reading. (Ask one or two students to share what their inner voice said and what they recorded.)

. . . Today we learned one more way our inner voice helps us notice when we read information that is new to us. We recorded the information. Then we coded it with . . . ? Right! An *L*.

. . . Let's look back at our chart to see if we need to add anything our inner voice might say when we read information new to us.

ASSESS AND PLAN

What did you notice about students' thinking as you listened to them read?

Noting new information is critical for students as they grow as readers. If students notice few new facts, it may be they aren't recognizing something as new. It may also indicate that the text is too easy or too difficult. Perhaps choose a different book about the same topic for the next session.

What did students write or draw on their Post-its?

Look through students' Post-its for evidence that they understand new information. Did they draw it? Did they put it into their own words, or did they just write down words from the text? We want to see evidence of authentic learning in students' responses. Incorporate additional modeling into the next session, or continue this session another day to model and support authentic learning.

[The comprehension] process is a constructive one that requires an active reader. (Almasi, 2003)

Integrate New Information

This session builds on the previous one. Students focus on merging their thinking with new information as they read.

Companion to . . .

The Primary Comprehension Toolkit
Lesson 7: Merge Thinking with New Learning

SESSION GOALS

We want students to:

- listen to the voice in their head that signals new learning.
- understand the term *background knowledge (BK)*.
- stop, think, and react to new information.
- mark Post-its with *L* (for *learn*) when they learn something new.

TEXT MATTERS

Consider how the text used in the previous session invited kids to recognize new learning. Select a new text if students finished the previous one.

A short article works well. "Seeing with Sound" in *Toolkit Texts: Grades 2–3* has enough information to engage kids in merging their background knowledge with new learning as they read.

CONSIDERATIONS FOR PLANNING

Continue working with kids on recognizing the inner voice that signals new learning. As you continue, students will see how to combine and merge their own thinking with new learning.

Have on hand the chart from the previous session (*My Inner Voice Says*). You will build on it in this session.

Build Background, Word and Concept Knowledge

- Continue to **focus on listening to the inner voice.** Shift more responsibility to students and allow them to spend most of the small-group time reading.

- Include some discussion about what readers do when they encounter new learning. **Explain that readers stop, think, and react** to new information.

. . . I know you are anxious to keep reading and looking for new information. Let's talk for just a minute about what we've been working on. Who can get us started? (We want kids to reconstruct the ideas of using background knowledge, noticing new learning, and merging their thinking with new information. Prompt as needed to review and recapture previous learning.)

. . . Today I want to show you something readers do when they find new information. They stop, think about the information, and sometimes have a response or reaction to it.

Teach/Model

- **Begin to read and model** how you stop, think, and react when you read something new.

- Remind kids how they listened to their inner voice when they encountered new information and facts. **Build on the chart** from the previous session. Using examples from the text, show kids how you merge your thinking with new information.

- **Model how you use visual and text features** to gain information and integrate it with information in the body text.

- As you model, find natural places where reading a new idea may cause a question to arise. **Demonstrate how you handle questions.**

. . . I am going to read a page to show you how I stop, think, and react when I read something new. Notice how I pay close attention to visual and text features that help me better understand the information.

. . . Ah, I hear my inner voice saying, "Wow! This is cool!" Now I'll think about how I merge my thinking with the information. (Create your own examples using the text. Use the chart from the previous session to show how you merge your thinking with new information. Add a new column with the heading *I Merge My Thinking with the Information*. Be sure to show kids how you handle a question.)

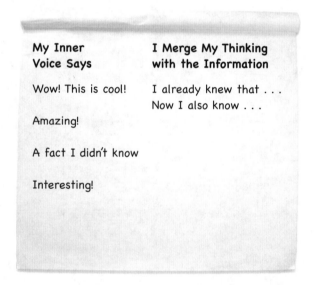

My Inner Voice Says	I Merge My Thinking with the Information
Wow! This is cool!	I already knew that . . . Now I also know . . .
Amazing!	
A fact I didn't know	
Interesting!	

. . . Today you're going to continue to read, listening to your inner conversation and using Post-its to record new learning. You're going to think about how what you read adds to what you already knew!

Guide/Support Practice

- **Have kids continue reading** and recording their new learning on Post-its.

- Move about the group, listening in to students' reading and thinking. **Provide support** and on-the-spot reteaching and modeling as needed.

. . . Let's read on. Use your Post-its to stop and record your new learning.

. . . I will be coming by to listen in on your reading and thinking.

Wrap Up

- **Ask students to share** their reactions.

- **Revisit the chart** to add any additional words or phrases kids heard their inner voices saying.

. . . Let's share some of the reactions you recorded. Did anyone have a question? Did anyone learn something new?

. . . You are learning so much about reading! Let's see if we can recall something we learned just now. (Add examples to the chart.)

. . . Remember to use this new learning as you keep reading on your own! Readers always think about what they will read next. Go ahead and choose a book you think you'd like to read from one of our nonfiction book baskets.

. . . Who would like to tell us about the book you chose? What do you think you will learn about?

. . . It seems like you have good reading plans!

ASSESS AND PLAN

What did you notice about students' understanding of background knowledge and its role in connecting new learning?
Think back to students' comments and also what students did as you listened in on each student's reading and thinking. Use read-aloud time with the whole group to continue to build on these important sessions.

Did you notice students who might need to be reminded to slow their reading down to note and react to new information?
Offer students ways to remind themselves to slow down and be more thoughtful. Sometimes it helps to give students a very small Post-it they can move to show the end of the "chunk" they will read before they stop, reflect, and consider any new information they encountered.

Reading Conference

Activate and Connect

After this unit, you want to know that students are consciously using what they know to understand, to make connections to their own lives, and to communicate information to others so your conference should help the student talk about his or her background knowledge in relation to new information. At the end of the conference is a brief interview focusing on the specialist teaching book the child created.

1. **Invite the student to choose a passage and create a context for it.**
   - Choose a part of your book to read to me.
   - *(If reading fiction)* Tell me what it's about.

2. *(If the student is reading fiction)* **Ask the student to make connections to personal experience.**
   - Tell me about a connection you made to your own life while reading. What did you hear your inner voice saying?
   - How did that connection help you better understand the story?

3. *(If the student is reading nonfiction)* **Ask the student to relate his or her background knowledge to new learning.**
   - Show me a part where you learned something new. What did you hear your inner voice saying as you read this part?
   - What did you know about this before you read this part?

4. **Ask the student to share and talk about his or her teaching book.**
   - Tell me about your teaching book—maybe you'd like to read me a page or two?
   - Tell me about some of the information you wanted to teach. Tell me something that you are really excited to teach your friends (and teachers).
   - Show me a text or visual feature you included. What information does it give you? Why did you include that photograph (illustration, chart, graph, map, etc.)?
   - How did you make sure the information in your book is accurate?

Reading Conference Recording Form: Activate and Connect	
Name _____ Date _____	
Book title _____	
GOAL	**EVIDENCE**
The student . . .	This student . . .
1. Understands the text • Tells what the book is about	
2. (If reading fiction) Uses connections to understand text • Makes connections to personal experience • Describes how connections furthered understanding of the text	
3. (If reading nonfiction) Activates background knowledge to understand new information • Notices and reacts when she or he learns something new • Relates background knowledge to new learning	
4. Shares teaching book • Enthusiastically shares information, visual and text features	

©2010 by Stephanie Harvey, Anne Goudvis, and Judy Wallis. From *Comprehension Intervention: Small-Group Lessons for The Primary Comprehension Toolkit.* Portsmouth, NH: Heinemann. This page may be copied for classroom use only.

Conference Recording Form for "Activate and Connect," located in "Resources" section.

Follow-Ups

If the student has difficulty with any of the primary goals in this unit, prompts like the following may be helpful during independent work in subsequent units.

- What do you already know about this topic?
- What does this remind you of?
- Did you remember to merge your thinking?
- What do you hear in your inner conversation?
- What did you learn that's new information?

Language students may use to demonstrate that they are using their background knowledge to connect new information to that which they know

- This reminds me of . . .
- I know . . .
- I noticed . . .
- I never knew . . .
- I learned . . .
- I used to think . . . Now I know . . .
- That feature helps me understand . . .

Ask Questions

Curiosity is at the heart of teaching and learning. Young kids burst through the door bubbling over with questions: "Why is the sky blue? Where does the sun go at night? What happened to the cowboys?" Questions spur curious minds to investigate. Questions open doors to understanding the world. When young readers read nonfiction and meet new information, they brim with questions. As we try to answer our questions, we discover new information and gain knowledge. Questions can spur further research and inquiry. Instead of demanding answers all the time, we need to teach kids to ask thoughtful and insightful questions. After all, if we hope to develop critical thinkers, we must teach our kids to think about and question what they listen to, read, and view. Asking questions enriches the learning experience and leads to deeper understanding. Questioning is the strategy that propels learners forward.

Good readers question and challenge authors as they read. (Block and Pressley, 2002)

Wonder about New Learning

In *The Primary Comprehension Toolkit* Lesson 8, students use an *I Learned/ I Wonder* thinksheet to build understanding as they read an article. The two companion sessions for Lesson 8 offer students more time and support to consider their background knowledge and clear up misconceptions as they read another text. In this first session, kids share what they think they know before they read. As they read, they record their new learning and questions on Post-its that they code and sort on personal *I Learned/I Wonder* charts.

Companion to ...

The Primary Comprehension Toolkit
Lesson 8: View and Read to Learn
and Wonder

TEXT MATTERS

Select a short text filled with interesting images and lots of great information to connect to, learn, and wonder about. Questions often arise in the midst of new learning.

"What's the Weather Out There" in *Keep Reading* has a question-answer text structure that will help kids see how their own questions work to push them on and keep them engaged. Selections such as "Ask the Farmer" in *Keep Reading* and "Shadows" and "Where Do I Live" in *Toolkit Texts: Grades 2–3* have enough information to allow kids to record new learning and questions.

SESSION GOALS

We want students to:

- use text and images to understand.
- think and wonder about new learning.
- jot down new learning and questions on Post-its and then sort them in two columns: *I Learned* and *I Wonder*.

CONSIDERATIONS FOR PLANNING

While questioning has often been an "after reading add-on" in comprehension instruction, we know that providing readers with opportunities to ask questions before, during, and after reading is important. The questions we ask help us organize and integrate new information and fuel further reading.

In this session, you will start a group chart: *What We Think We Know/ What We Learned*. Kids will share what they *think* they know about the topic before they read. In the next session, they will share what they learned and clear up misconceptions.

Students will need Post-its and personal *I Learned/I Wonder* charts.

Build Background, Word and Concept Knowledge

- **Engage kids by sharing the cover** of the book or magazine you've selected. If using a text with no cover, have kids look at the title and visuals.

- **Ask kids what they think they know** about the topic. Create a *What We Think We Know/ What We Learned* chart. Record both accurate ideas and misconceptions in the first column. In the next session, you will help kids use the second column.

- **Review the concepts** of *background knowledge* and *accuracy*.

- **Introduce the term *misconception*.** Explain that we fix our misconceptions as we read and learn new information.

- **In the next session,** we will revisit the chart, add what students learned, and clear up their misconceptions.

Teaching Tip

Model and think aloud to show kids how important it is for all readers to wonder and ask questions that help them clear up misconceptions. We encourage kids to get excited about something that helps us revise or change our thinking.

. . . I have a great text for us to read! Take a look! I'll bet you have wondered about _____ (topic). What do you know about _____? Turn and talk.

. . . Let's hear some of the things you think you know. I'll record them on a chart.

What We Think We Know	What We Learned

. . . Does anyone remember what we call what we already know? Yes, *background knowledge.* You have some interesting background knowledge about this topic.

. . . Remember how we talked about accuracy in nonfiction books? What does *accurate* mean? Right! It means something is correct, or true.

. . . Well, sometimes we have background knowledge that *isn't* accurate. As we read, we get a chance to learn more and correct what we don't understand. We call ideas that turn out not to be accurate *misconceptions.* It is super-important to fix our misconceptions!

. . . We will come back to this chart after we finish reading. We'll see if we've changed our thinking about anything we thought we knew.

Teach /Model

- During this session, we show kids that when we learn new information, we often wonder about it. To help kids understand the difference between new learning and wondering, **use an I Learned/I Wonder chart.** A form is provided in *The Primary Comprehension Toolkit Strategy Book 3: Ask Questions,* page 69, or you can make your own.

- **Model your own reading,** making your thinking explicit by coding Post-its with an *L* for *learn* or a *?* for *wonder* and placing them in the appropriate column on the chart.

- **Include visual and text features** in your modeling so kids continue to see that the features are important sources of information.

- **Preview vocabulary** that may be new to students. Model how you use the context and your background knowledge to make sense of these words.

. . . We have been using Post-its to note information that is new as we read. Remember, we put an *L* on our Post-its when we *learn* something.

. . . Today I will show you how I use Post-its to keep track of what I learn *and* what I wonder. I'm going to code my Post-its and put them on a chart. This is my *I Learned/I Wonder* chart.

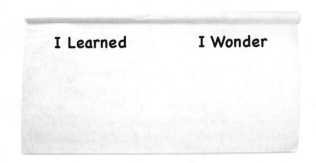

. . . What is the title of our text? What do you think we might learn from reading this? Turn and talk. (Engage kids in discussion.)

. . . I am going to start reading. As I read, I will think about how I use my background knowledge to understand new information. I'll also think about how, sometimes, what I read or see causes me to *wonder* about something. We already know how to code what we *learn* with an *L.* We will use a question mark to code when we *wonder: ?.* Let me show you. (Model just enough to be sure that students know exactly what to do.)

. . . Let's talk about some words you'll need to know as you read on. Here's one . . .

Guide/Support Practice

TEACHING MOVES

- **Have kids read and record** on their own. Give them paper and Post-its to create their own *I Learned/I Wonder* charts. Offer support as needed.

- **Look for misconceptions** that you might need to clarify for the group during the wrap up or at the beginning of the next session.

TEACHING LANGUAGE

. . . It's time for you to read now. I'll give you Post-its and paper to make your own chart. Let's write *I Learned/I Wonder* at the top of the chart. (Or give kids a copy of the chart.)

. . . Let's help one another. Who can remember exactly what we should do? Great!

. . . I will listen in on your reading and thinking, so if you have questions, I will be ready to answer them.

Wrap Up

TEACHING MOVES

- **Have kids share** their *I Learned/I Wonder* charts.

- **The following session** will provide time to look for misconceptions and help students see that sometimes our learning changes our background knowledge.

TEACHING LANGUAGE

. . . Let's look at your charts. Turn and talk about what you wrote. Wow, look at what you know and what you still wonder about!

. . . We will put our charts and our reading together the next time we meet.

. . . The things you learned have increased your background knowledge—you know more than you did when you started to read!

ASSESS AND PLAN

Did students recognize the difference between the *I Learned* and *I Wonder* columns?

If students don't understand the different purposes for the two columns, spend additional time in the next session clarifying how they are different and why each is important.

Did students use visual and text features as sources of information?

If students didn't reference the visual or text features, be sure to provide an additional model. Kids encounter more and more features in higher levels of text, so it is important for them to recognize the features as important sources of information.

Check to make sure:

- students understand the difference between a fact (I learned) and a question (I wonder).
- students' reactions and responses are authentic—a question they really wonder about, or a genuine reaction to new learning.
- students are using their knowledge of visual and text features to think about new information.

> *We need to support students in becoming more self-sustaining, thoughtful, independent readers and writers.* (Routman, 2003)

Companion to . . .

The Primary Comprehension Toolkit
Lesson 8: View and Read to Learn and Wonder

SESSION GOALS

We want students to:

- use text and images to understand.
- think and wonder about new learning.
- jot down new learning and questions on Post-its and then sort them into two columns: *I Learned* and *I Wonder*.
- understand that misconceptions are normal and that learners revise their thinking after reading and listening to additional information.

Use New Learning to Revise Thinking

This session builds on the previous one. Students use their personal *I Learned/I Wonder* charts to check the group chart of background knowledge, correct misconceptions, and record new learning.

TEXT MATTERS

Continue using the short text from the previous session. Be sure that students are using the visual and text features in identifying the things they learn and the things they wonder about.

CONSIDERATIONS FOR PLANNING

If students still seem unclear about identifying what is new learning and what is a related question or something they wonder, take time to review and model.

The texts students read not only increase their background knowledge, they also ensure students amend misconceptions. This session will focus on any misconceptions students identified in their own background knowledge as they read.

You will need the group's *What We Think We Know/What We Learned* chart from the previous session.

Students will need their personal *I Learned/I Wonder* charts from the previous session.

Build Background, Word and Concept Knowledge

- **Ask kids to review** what they did in the previous session.

- **Review the term *misconceptions*.** Explain that all of us have misconceptions, and when we read more about a topic, we correct our misunderstanding by revising our thinking.

- Tell kids they will **use their personal charts to check the group chart** and revise any misconceptions.

. . . Let's think back. Who can remind us of what we learned and did?

. . . Right! Each of you created a personal chart, *I Learned/I Wonder*, and you put your Post-its in one column or the other.

. . . Remember, we also talked about being *accurate* and fixing up our *misconceptions*, or our *mis*understandings! All of us have misperceptions, and sometimes what we learn helps us *revise*, or change, our thinking.

. . . We will look back at our group chart, *What We Think We Know/What We Learned*, to see if we need to revise any misconceptions.

Teach/Model

- **Have kids look over their personal charts** to look for learning that might help correct any misconceptions.

- **Analyze the group list,** *What We Think We Know*, to identify any misconceptions. Add the accurate information to the chart.

. . . Look over your personal *I Learned/I Wonder* charts. Turn and talk about what you learned.

. . . Let's look back now at the chart we made right before we started to read. Does anyone see something we *thought* we knew that isn't accurate? (Have kids identify anything that might be a misconception and correct it by adding something they learned. See example.)

What We Think We Know	What We Learned
~~Fish have lungs.~~	Fish use gills to breathe.

. . . Wow! We knew lots about _____ before we read, but we also found out we needed to change some of what we *thought* we knew. It's important to be accurate.

. . . Let's keep on reading and adding to our chart.

Guide/Support Practice

TEACHING MOVES

- **Have kids read** and add to their charts. Spend extra time as needed with any student who seems confused.

TEACHING LANGUAGE

. . . Time for you to read now. Keep adding to your charts.

. . . I will listen in on your reading and thinking.

Wrap Up

TEACHING MOVES

- **Have kids share** their personal charts again and talk about new Post-its they have added.

- **Revisit the group chart** and revise any misconceptions.

TEACHING LANGUAGE

. . . Let's look at our charts. Turn and talk about what you wrote. Wow, look at what you added!

. . . We should look back at our group chart to see if we need to correct anything in it. Is there any information that we need to fix?

. . . You have done a great job today! Let's think about what we learned.

Assess and Plan

Did students understand the concepts of *misconception* and *accuracy?*
Some students will find it difficult to revise their thinking. If they have had the misconception for some time, it may be difficult for them to replace the inaccurate information with accurate facts.

Do students see misconceptions as a normal part of learning and understand that reading is a powerful way to add to and revise their background knowledge?
Continue to build on the powerful concept that all of us have misconceptions and that they are a natural part of learning. We encourage kids to get excited about something that helps us revise or change our thinking.

> *In brief, the function of knowledge is to make one experience freely available to other experiences.*
> (Dewey, 1916)

Companion to . . .

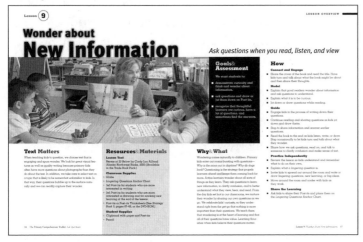

The Primary Comprehension Toolkit
Lesson 9: Wonder about New Information

SESSION GOALS

We want students to:

■ demonstrate curiosity and think and wonder about information.

■ ask questions and draw or jot them down on Post-its.

■ recognize that thoughtful learners are curious, have a lot of questions, and sometimes find the answers.

Ask Questions As You Read

In *The Primary Comprehension Toolkit* Lesson 9, students ask and answer questions as they read, listen, and view a nonfiction read-aloud. This companion session offers students more time and support to ask and answer questions as they read another text.

TEXT MATTERS

Engaging, interesting texts are essential when teaching students to wonder and question. Select a text on a topic your students are curious about. Choose one with interesting features that will support inquiry and new learning.

Articles such as "Whose Feet Are Whose?" from *Toolkit Texts: Grades 2–3* and "Prairie Dog Homes" from *Keep Reading* have enough information to prompt kids to wonder, ask questions, and find some answers as they read.

Kids also need to read and explore books brimming with things they want to learn—nonfiction books that have engaging covers, interesting titles, photographs, charts, and other features. For independent reading, provide books like *Where Butterflies Grow* by Joanne Ryder and *What's Out There: A Book About Space* by Lynn Wilson.

CONSIDERATIONS FOR PLANNING

Young children have dozens of questions. They love wondering about the world around them. We show kids how using their curiosity to ask and answer questions can help them grow as readers.

Good readers wonder and ask questions as they read. They often stop to think before they read on. This session focuses on helping kids identify their questions and use them to better understand the text.

Students will need Post-its for this session.

Build Background, Word and Concept Knowledge

- **Talk about the word** *curious* and what it means to wonder.

- Explain to kids that it is natural to be curious—to be eager to learn something. Good readers read because they are interested and want to learn. Sometimes **reading causes us to wonder and ask questions** that help us better understand the text.

- Explain that not all questions are answered as we read. **Introduce the term** *lingering* **questions.**

. . . Have you ever heard something that made you curious? Perhaps you heard something really interesting, and when you thought about it more, you began to wonder. Has that happened to you?

. . . Being *curious* is being eager to learn. Curiosity is what causes us to ask questions, and it is a BIG part of reading and learning. In fact, it is so important because when we read with a question in our mind, we are looking for the answer. Many of our questions do get answered!

. . . There are other times when we finish a book and we still have questions. We call those questions *lingering* questions.

Teach/Model

- With the text cover hidden, **tell students the title and invite them to turn and talk,** thinking about the topic of the text.

- **Preview any vocabulary** kids will need to know.

- **Continue looking through the text** and prompting for what kids are noticing and wondering. Stop and discuss visual and text features.

- **Model reading, wondering, and recording questions.** Write and/or draw several of your questions on Post-its.

- Remind kids that they may have some **lingering questions** that don't get answered as they read.

. . . I have this book (or article). Without showing you the cover, I am going to tell you the title . . . . Wow, pretty interesting, right? What do you suppose the text is about? Turn and talk.

. . . Good thinking! Let's talk about some words you'll need to know when we read . . .

. . . Let's continue looking at the book (or article). So often in the last few weeks, I have noticed that as we read and view new information, our curiosity leads us to have questions or things we wonder about.

. . . Let me show you how I keep track of my questions as I read and view. Right here as I read this part, I am wondering, "What . . . ?" I will write that down on a Post-it. Here I have a question, too. I wonder . . . This time I will draw a picture and add a question mark, *?*, to my Post-it to show I have a question.

. . . As I read on, my questions won't always be answered. Who remembers what we call those kinds of questions? Right, *lingering* questions!

Guide/Support Practice

TEACHING MOVES

- **Read a page or section together** and guide kids in writing down a question or two before they begin reading themselves.

- **Have students continue to read** and record their questions on Post-its.

TEACHING LANGUAGE

. . . As I read this next page, jot or draw something you wonder about.

. . . Who has something you can share?

. . . I am going to give each of you several Post-its so you can continue to write down your questions. I will be listening in on your reading.

Wrap Up

TEACHING MOVES

- **Invite students to share** their Post-its.

- **Have kids share lingering questions.** If they haven't recorded one, have them make a Post-it of something they still wonder.

- **Make a *Lingering Questions* chart.** Have students note questions they still have and put their Post-its on the chart.

- Explain that **lingering questions can lead to further reading** and investigation.

TEACHING LANGUAGE

. . . Who would like to share one of your questions? . . . And did you find an answer? Tell us about what you learned.

. . . Who wondered about something but didn't find the answer? Let's hear your question. Remember, we can't always answer our questions, and that's okay!

. . . Everyone take a minute to think about something you still wonder. If you don't already have it written down, write or draw it on a Post-it.

. . . Let's talk about what we are still wondering. As you share, we'll put your lingering questions on our *Lingering Questions* anchor chart.

. . . These kinds of questions cause us to investigate and read more. It feels great to find answers when we wonder and read on.

Assess and Plan

Did students demonstrate curiosity and engage in wondering and questioning?

Asking thoughtful questions takes time and doesn't always come naturally. As teachers, we have many opportunities to model the kinds of thinking we want kids to do. One of the most helpful ways to encourage kids to ask high-quality questions is to pause and point out good questions as kids ask them throughout the day.

Did students have thoughtful questions?

Kids are natural questioners. Our role as teachers is to leverage students' curiosity and help them use it to strengthen their reading. Read-alouds afford us many opportunities to model. Consider asking kids to come to their small reading group with something they are wondering about. They will hear all kinds of questions and expand how they use questions in their own reading.

Questions tend to be generative, leading to more thinking. (Keene and Zimmermann, 2007)

Record Questions and Answers

In *The Primary Comprehension Toolkit* Lesson 10, students jot down their questions and answers on a thinksheet as they read. The three sessions supporting Lesson 10 help students break down this process. In this first session, they use Post-its to record their questions and write the answers if they find them.

TEXT MATTERS

Nonfiction texts about interesting topics invite kids' questions and cause them to wonder. Select a text that has photographs or illustrations with captions and other text features. Headings are particularly good because they provoke questioning.

Companion to . . .

The Primary Comprehension Toolkit
Lesson 10: Use Questions as Tools for Learning

Consider using a book like *Eyes* by Elizabeth Miles (*Animal Parts* series) or *Bats* by Patricia Whitehouse (*What's Awake* series). You will continue with the same text in the next session.

A short article also works well. "Animal Helpers" in *Toolkit Texts: Grades 2–3* and "What's the Weather Out There?" and "How Seeds Spread" in *Keep Reading* have enough information to prompt kids to ask questions and find some answers as they read. In the next session, they will reread and read on if they haven't finished.

SESSION GOAL

We want students to:

- stop, wonder, and keep a question in mind to try to answer it.

CONSIDERATIONS FOR PLANNING

This session builds on Session 9 and extends how kids use questions to fuel their reading. Reading "with a question in mind" keeps kids actively engaged in reading. While readers may identify an overall purpose for reading, the questions they ask *during* reading promote purposeful reading.

We want kids to pause during reading to ask questions and wonder, and to read on with those questions as their guide.

Students will need Post-its.

Build Background, Word and Concept Knowledge

TEACHING MOVES

- **Review the importance of being curious.** Remind kids that being curious causes us to want to find out things that interest us. It creates questions in our minds. Our questions contribute to a better understanding of the text.

- **Pull out and discuss or ask questions about vocabulary** that may be unfamiliar. It's important to show kids how to ask questions about unknown or unfamiliar words.

TEACHING LANGUAGE

. . . When we met last, we talked about being curious. Who can remember what that word *curious* means? Right! Being curious is being eager to find out about the world and learn something!

. . . When we are curious, we ask questions. And you know something *really* interesting? The more we learn, the more questions we have!

. . . Some words might be new to you when we read today. Here's one . . .

Teach/Model

TEACHING MOVES

- **Show the cover** of the book or the title of the article. Invite kids to share any questions they immediately have.

- **Model how you read** and pay attention to your inner voice. Tell students that you are thinking aloud and sharing what your inner voice is saying.

- **When you have a question, record it on a Post-it.** When you find an answer in the text, show kids how you return to your question, write the answer, and move the Post-it to the place where you found the answer.

TEACHING LANGUAGE

. . . Let's look at the cover of the book (or title of the article). I can tell that you already have questions in your head! I know I do. I am wondering . . . (offer an example).

. . . Turn and talk about a question you have. (Give kids time to generate some questions.) Let's share some of the questions.

. . . Let me show you how I read, asking questions. Remember, your inner voice alerts you. You will hear your inner voice saying, "I am wondering . . ." Watch as I read.

. . . I have a question here . . . I am going to write my question on a Post-it. (Continue reading. If you find the answer, write it on the same Post-it, explaining that you will place the Post-it next to the part where your question was answered.)

. . . Turn and talk about what you notice me doing as I read. (Ask kids to share what they noticed.)

Guide/Support Practice

- **Read a page or section together.** Guide kids in identifying and writing down a question or two before they begin reading themselves.

- **Have kids read,** using Post-its to keep track of their questions and answers.

. . . Let's do the next one together. (Kids read and identify a question.)

. . . I am going to give each of you some Post-its so you can continue to write down your questions. Remember, if you find an answer to your question, you will put it on your Post-it and place your Post-it right beside the answer in the text.

Wrap Up

- **Invite kids to share** some of their Post-its.

- **If kids completed the text,** have them keep their unanswered questions on the inside of the cover or on the back of the short article. They will use those questions in the next sessions.

- **Create an anchor chart** with students to help them recall the process. You will continue to build onto this chart during the next two sessions.

When We Read with a Question in Mind

1. We ask a question.
2. We read on to see if our question is answered.

. . . Who would like to share one of your questions? . . . And did you find an answer?

. . . Turn and talk about what you found. (Have kids share some of their questions.)

. . . I see you put Post-its right next to the part of the text where you found answers.

. . . Some of you finished the text and still have questions you didn't find the answer to. If you didn't find an answer, I want you to save your Post-its like this. (Have kids place them inside the cover or on the back of the article.)

. . . Let's make a chart to help us remember what we do when we read with a question in mind. First, we ask a question. I'll write that on the chart.

. . . What do we do next? (Prompt kids to record that they read on to see if the question is answered in the text.)

. . . We will learn more and add to our chart the next time we meet.

ASSESS AND PLAN

Did students stop, wonder, and keep a question in their mind to answer as they read?

Make sure kids understand that the questions we ask fuel our reading. Knowing how to adjust their reading to stop and wonder is a difficult concept for kids. They may be accustomed to just "plowing ahead" in their reading. You may want to offer additional modeling to ensure they understand how to adjust their reading to accommodate questions.

Use Strategies to Find Answers

Energy and curiosity make good deskmates. (Ashton-Warner, 1974)

This second session builds on the previous one. Students identify unanswered questions and search for answers by looking at visual features and asking peers.

Companion to . . .

The Primary Comprehension Toolkit
Lesson 10: Use Questions as Tools for Learning

TEXT MATTERS

Continue using the text from the previous session. Students will reread portions of the text and read on if they haven't completed the text.

Provide books children can choose from for their independent reading. We keep lots of wonderful nonfiction books in baskets to encourage students to read independently.

CONSIDERATIONS FOR PLANNING

The goal of this session is to help kids see that pictures as well as words offer information, and they need to use both as readers to gain understanding. The session introduces the important idea that learning is social. We encourage kids to talk to peers when a text doesn't answer a question they have.

You will need the anchor chart from Session 10a.

Students will need the text with their unanswered questions from Session 10a.

SESSION GOAL

We want students to:
- learn strategies for answering questions, including gaining information from pictures as well as text and talking with peers.

Build Background, Word and Concept Knowledge

- **Have students review** what they did in the previous session. Refer to the anchor chart you started. (Kids thought of a question, wrote it on a Post-it, and looked for an answer as they read on. Then they put the answer on the Post-it and placed the Post-it next to the answer they found in the text.)

- **Ask kids to share questions** that were answered and questions that weren't.

. . . Let's look back at our reading. (Have students look at the text they read during the previous session.)

. . . Someone start us off. Tell us what we did when we read this text. (As students recall the process, refer to the anchor chart. If kids mention additional things, add those to the anchor chart.)

. . . Right! We learned to listen to our inner voice when it said, "I wonder," "What if . . . ?" or "I don't understand."

. . . Who would like to share a question that was answered in the text?

. . . What about a question that *wasn't* answered? Who can share one of those?

Teach/Model

- **Look back through the text** to find a place where you had a question.

- **Model how you use pictures** to add to your understanding. Explain that visual features often contain information that helps us answer questions.

- **Write the answer on your Post-it** and place it beside the illustration.

- **Model how readers sometimes talk** and share background knowledge to get their questions answered.

- **Keep track of things to add to the anchor chart** started in the previous session.

> **Teaching Tip**
> One of the most difficult aspects of reading nonfiction is learning how to integrate the text with the visual features. We teach kids by showing them how we read, pause, look at the visual, and combine information from both the text and the visual to deepen our understanding.

. . . We are going to learn how we don't use only the words to help us understand, but we also use the pictures. Let's look back at the text we read.

. . . Look at this picture (point to a specific picture). I remember reading here that . . . I found the words really interesting, but when I look at this picture, I find out lots more information.

. . . Let me show you how I read the text and also "read" the picture. Sometimes the pictures cause me to wonder just as the words do.

. . . When I read this part, I had a question. But I looked at the picture, and it answered my question. (Write the question on the Post-it and then add the answer. Place the Post-it near the illustration.)

. . . Turn and talk about what you notice I do as I read. (Ask kids to share what they noticed.)

. . . Before you try this, I want to share one more way we can get our questions answered. We can talk to one another!

. . . When we made our teaching books, I discovered that we have a (dinosaur) specialist in our group! (Choose a topic that fits the text.) So, if I have an unanswered question, I can ask her to share her background knowledge.

Guide/Support Practice

- **Guide kids** in finding a place where they had an unanswered question. When they locate one, have them look at any nearby illustrations or visuals that might help them.

- **Have students continue to reread,** looking at both the text and the visuals. It is likely they will find answers they missed in their first reading.

- If the visual doesn't help in answering the question, **suggest that students consult a peer.**

- **If kids have not completed the text,** have them read on.

. . . Now let's try it together. Spread out the questions you weren't able to answer. Find the part in the text where you had that question. Let's see now if there is a picture nearby that helps to answer it.

. . . Anyone find an answer? (Have kids share how using the visual information helps them.)

. . . What if your question is still unanswered? Right! We can ask the group. Who has an unanswered question you'd like to ask the group? (Have kids share several questions. While some questions will remain unanswered, students learn yet another way to get their questions answered.)

Wrap Up

- **Invite kids to share** any new questions they have.

- **Keep track of lingering questions.** Students will use them in the next session.

- **Revisit the chart.** Have kids discuss their new learning and add it to the chart.

When We Read with a Question in Mind

1. We ask a question.
2. We read on to see if our question is answered.
3. We use pictures, too, to see if they answer our questions.
4. We can talk with others and ask them to share their background knowledge with us.

- **Have kids choose a book** to read independently. Give them Post-its to record their questions and answers.

. . . Does anyone have any new questions to share?

. . . Remember, we are keeping track of our lingering questions. Keep them inside the cover or on the back of your text. We'll talk more about them next time we meet.

. . . What important things did we learn today that we might add to our chart? (Prompt students as needed to add that they look at the pictures and talk to someone.)

. . . Now I want you to choose an information book from one of the baskets. Make sure it is "just right" for you. Use what we have been learning about asking questions when you read. Here are some Post-its to use. Bring your new thinking back to our next meeting.

ASSESS AND PLAN

Did students seem confident using both words and visuals to answer their questions?

Moving between the text and visual information is often challenging. Students may need additional modeling one-on-one. The modeling done by the teacher, along with guided support, followed by coaching the student during reading, will help promote learning.

Look over students' questions and answers in their books. Do you see any misconceptions, or places where students might have misinterpreted or misunderstood the text?

Confer individually with any student who has a misconception. We want to make sure students accurately build their background knowledge.

> *To be able to ask questions, students must be actively thinking about and working with the text.*
> (Mason and Au, 1986)

Companion to . . .

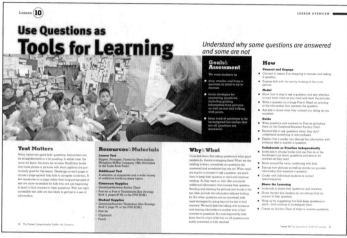

The Primary Comprehension Toolkit
Lesson 10: Use Questions as Tools
for Learning

SESSION GOAL

We want students to:

- keep track of questions to be investigated but realize not all questions are answered.

Find Answers Beyond the Text

This third session builds on the previous two. Students record questions that are still unanswered, review strategies they've tried, and consider where to look next.

TEXT MATTERS

Continue using the text from the previous session. Students will reread portions of the text or read on if they haven't completed the text.

CONSIDERATIONS FOR PLANNING

The goal of this session is to help kids see that they can reread, read on, use pictures, or talk to others to answer their questions. They also learn that questions do not always have answers.

You will need the anchor chart from Session 10b.

Students will need the text with their lingering questions from Session 10b.

Build Background, Word and Concept Knowledge

- **Revisit the text** from the previous session and ask kids what they did to find answers to their questions.

- **Use the anchor chart** to support discussion.

When We Read with a Question in Mind

1. We ask a question.
2. We read on to see if our question is answered.
3. We use pictures, too, to see if they answer our questions.
4. We can talk with others and ask them to share their background knowledge with us.

- **Have kids share lingering questions.** They will be the focus of this session.

Teaching Tip

Some students may have answered a question inaccurately by misinterpreting or misunderstanding the text. This happens to all of us. As you review questions and answers, model how to check for accuracy.

. . . Let's look back at our reading. (Have students look at the text.)

. . . Remember we have learned several ways we can get answers to the questions we have as we read. Who can name one of the ways we find answers? (Use the anchor chart to support discussion and review.)

. . . Who can share a question that was answered in the text? What about a question that *wasn't* answered? We had some of those, didn't we? That's what we will talk about now—those unanswered, *lingering* questions!

Teach/Model

- In this session, we show students that **not all questions can be answered** in their current text or even with the help of someone else. They may need to investigate in other texts or resources.

- **Show kids how to make a chart** that will help them think about their lingering questions.

- **Model how to use the chart.** Read a question on a Post-it. Look back through the text and check the words and pictures to see if the question actually might have been answered. This demonstrates how we read in flexible ways.

- **Reinforce the need for accuracy.** We want kids to look for and revise any misconceptions.

- **If the question isn't answered,** save it on the chart. Think about where you can look for an answer, and jot down your ideas.

. . . We are going to learn what happens when we can't find answers to our questions in the text.

. . . I am going to give you a sheet of paper. (Use the paper landscape so there's room to write.) At the top, write *My UNanswered Questions*. (Model how to write the title.) Put your Post-its with lingering questions on the chart. (Kids can also use the back of the paper.)

. . . I had a question that didn't get answered. (Model, using your question.) Before I put it on my chart, I am going to read back through the text and look at the pictures to see if I might have missed something. I am going to ask you, too. (When the question isn't answered, put it on the chart.)

. . . I didn't find the answer, so I am going to show on my chart that I checked the words and pictures.

. . . Finally, I am going to think of where I might look to investigate and find my answer. (List ideas for where you will look next: another book, the Internet, a "specialist.")

. . . Turn and talk about what you are noticing.

Guide/Support Practice

TEACHING MOVES

■ **Guide kids** in considering their own unanswered questions. Have them look back at the words and visuals, quickly rereading. During the wrap-up, you'll have students ask one another.

TEACHING LANGUAGE

. . . Now you try it. Who wants to tell the group how to start? (Make sure students know exactly what to do.)

. . . I will be around to help you.

. . . Remember to reread to be sure you haven't missed something.

Wrap Up

TEACHING MOVES

■ **Revisit the chart** and add the new learning.

**When We Read
with a Question in Mind**

1. We ask a question.
2. We read on to see if our question is answered.
3. We use pictures, too, to see if they answer our questions.
4. We can talk with others and ask them to share their background knowledge with us.
5. When we can't answer a question, we investigate by reading further, looking online, asking a specialist, etc.

TEACHING LANGUAGE

. . . Wow! We have learned lots about reading with a question in our mind!

. . . Let's reread our chart. (For young children, offer a pointer to help in rereading.)

. . . What can we add to the chart to capture what we learned today?

. . . Great work! Now you have lots of new ways to keep growing what you know!

ASSESS AND PLAN

Did any students have difficulty?

If you observed a student who found any part of the process difficult, confer with the student individually. Have the student think aloud as he reads, explaining what he is doing and thinking and why. You will often see exactly where confusion occurs, and you can model, coach, and provide feedback.

Throw open the library, the delight of discovery is a major pleasure of reading.
(Stegner, 1988)

Companion to . . .

The Primary Comprehension Toolkit
Lesson 11: Read with a Question in Mind

Use a Table of Contents to Find Answers

In *The Primary Comprehension Toolkit* Lesson 11, students learn practical ways to navigate informational texts by using a table of contents, key words, and other features to locate information that answers their questions. The two companion sessions for Lesson 11 offer students more support for using navigational features to find answers. In this first session, they focus on using a table of contents.

Text Matters

Navigational features such as headings, a table of contents, and an index support readers in their quest to answer questions and find specific information. This session focuses on helping students learn how to use a table of contents.

Select a short, accessible book, such as *Spiders* by Monica Hughes or *Spiders* by Gail Gibbons, that has a clear, straightforward table of contents that will be easy for kids to use. If the book also has headings, you may continue using it in the next session.

Have a basketful of books available for browsing. While kids will study specific features in their small group, it is important to offer additional books so they can read, explore, and use features on their own. You may even invite kids to leave their "footprints" in a book by placing Post-its with questions they had as they read. This will encourage readers to seek out others to share and receive information.

Considerations for Planning

Our goal is to help kids see how they can use the navigational features of a text to help them read productively with a question in mind. In this session, we show kids how using a table of contents helps us read efficiently when we have a question.

Students will need personal *I Wonder/I Learned* charts.

Students will need Post-its.

Session Goals

We want students to:
- keep a question in mind as they read to answer it.
- use navigational features of texts to find answers to their questions.
- focus on using a table of contents.

Build Background, Word and Concept Knowledge

- Students need to **see their own questions as fuel for inquiry and research.** When questions are personal, they are also meaningful. When kids are encouraged and supported in asking and answering questions, they develop efficacy and agency.

- **Introduce the term** *table of contents*. In this session we will show kids how navigational features such as a table of contents help readers locate information that answers their questions.

. . . We have been talking about questions that we think of as we read.

. . . When we look through a nonfiction book, we immediately think of things we want to know. Our inner voice helps us identify things we wonder about as we preview the text.

. . . Good readers use their questions to "power" their reading. Just as a car needs gas to go, readers use questions to fuel reading. Good readers select texts that answer their questions. Sometimes their reading prompts new questions, too!

. . . A new term we'll be using today is *table of contents*. Does anyone know what a table of contents is? Right! A table of contents lists the "contents," or what you will find in the book and where it is located. It is a really handy feature in informational books.

Teach/Model

- **Look through the text together.** Show students that when we preview a text, we see photographs and other visuals that immediately cause us to wonder. We want kids to ask authentic questions—questions that will help them expand their growing knowledge.

- **Have kids share and write their questions** on Post-its.

- **Introduce the chart.** Post a student's question on the *I Wonder* side of the chart.

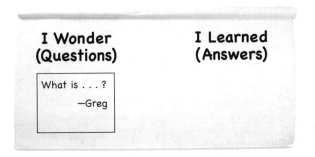

- **Model how you skim and scan the table of contents** to locate the most likely place to begin looking for the information.

- **As you find and read information,** record the answers on the *I Learned* side of the chart, using bullets (another text feature) to list the answers.

- **Show how you shorten the information,** keeping only the most important ideas. Explain that bullets help organize information so it is clear and easy to understand.

. . . Let's look together at this book. I'll turn the pages slowly. Look at the great photographs. Here's what I know about . . . (Share a little of your own background knowledge.)

. . . Some of these pictures are amazing, and I immediately think of questions I have—things I'd like to know.

. . . Turn and talk about your own questions— things you are wondering. Write your questions on Post-its. (Read and talk about kids' questions.)

. . . Now I'll show you how I keep a question in mind as I read. I will use a chart to help me keep track of my questions. (Introduce the chart and post questions as you proceed.)

. . . Let's try to answer some of our questions. We'll see if we can answer (Greg's) question.

. . . Instead of looking through the whole book, I am going to use the table of contents. Remember, this great feature helps us when we are reading with a specific question in mind.

. . . I'll keep (Greg's) question in mind as I scan the table of contents. (Think aloud as you scan.) Ah, I think this might be a good place to start. Let's turn to page . . . to see if we find the information.

. . . As I read, notice what I do and say. (As you find answers, list them on the chart.) I am going to write information that answers our question. I'll write what we read but make it shorter to get just the main ideas, or the most important information. I'll use bullets to keep all the information straight. Watch how I record the information.

. . . What did you notice me doing?

Guide/Support Practice

- **Have kids read and use the chart** to record their questions and answers.

- **Remind them to use the table of contents** to help them decide where to read and look for information.

- **Guide and support** students as needed.

. . . I am going to give you your own *I Wonder/ I Learned* chart.

. . . Now you select one of your own questions to answer. Remember to use the table of contents to help you find information in the text.

. . . I will be around to listen and help.

Wrap Up

- **Have kids share** from their charts. Reinforce for kids that our questions create an authentic purpose for reading. As we read, we discover things we wonder about. As we wonder, we read to answer our questions and clarify our thinking.

- Reinforce that using **a table of contents helps us find information** in the text.

- **Note any unanswered questions** kids have. In the next session, we show students how to use headings to find information. You may continue with the same book or select a new text.

. . . Let's take a look at your charts. Who found an answer to a question you had? (Have students share a few questions and their answers.)

. . . Great work today! You've learned something really important. Good readers work smartly! Using the table of contents often helps us to find answers to our questions with ease.

. . . Does anyone have a question that didn't get answered today?

ASSESS AND PLAN

Were students able to use their questions and the table of contents to find answers?

Some students may need extra support in using the table of contents. Since the table of contents may not have the exact wording as the questions they have written, kids may need additional modeling to show how we look where we think we'll find the information we need.

What other navigational features would help kids read the text productively with their questions in mind?

The next session helps kids use headings. A similar session can be organized around other navigational features of texts, such as the index.

Kids pursuing their own questions often discover many intriguing lines of thought to explore. (Keene, 2008)

Use Headings to Find Answers

This second session builds on the previous one. Students read the text, using headings to locate information that answers their questions.

Companion to . . .

The Primary Comprehension Toolkit
Lesson 11: Read with a Question in Mind

SESSION GOALS

We want students to:

- keep a question in mind as they read to answer it.
- use navigational features of texts to find answers to their questions.
- focus on using headings.

TEXT MATTERS

In the previous session, students used the table of contents to read with a specific question in mind. If the book has headings, you can continue with the same text so students have an opportunity to read the entire book and use other features.

A short article with headings also works well. "Aim for the Stars" in *Toolkit Texts: Grades 2–3* and "What's the Weather Out There?" in *Keep Reading* have headings and other features that will help kids navigate the text and locate information.

CONSIDERATIONS FOR PLANNING

The goal of this session is to help students see how they can read with a question in mind and use navigational features such as headings to find answers. Consider any lingering questions kids may have from the previous session.

Students will need their *I Wonder/I Learned* charts from the previous session or a new chart if you are using a new text.

Build Background, Word and Concept Knowledge

TEACHING MOVES

- **Review what kids did** in the previous session.

- **Introduce the term _headings_.** Many nonfiction texts include headings as organizers. In this session, we will show kids how to use headings to find information and meaning. Reading with a question in mind, they can use a heading as a signal that a question they have with similar words will likely be answered within that chunk of text.

TEACHING LANGUAGE

. . . We have been talking about questions that we think of as we read. We already thought of some questions and used the table of contents to seek answers.

. . . Now we will use another navigational feature: _headings._ Just as we use street signs to find our way around town, readers use headings like this (show an example) to get their questions answered and successfully arrive at their destination: understanding!

Teach/Model

- **Introduce the text and the term *headings*.** Show kids that when we look at informational text, we often see lines in bold type, called headings. Headings are like street signs or previews; they help us find our way through the text.

- **Invite kids to continue asking questions** and using their questions to expand their growing knowledge. Using headings offers them one more tool on their journey as a reader.

- Model how you **use a heading to find information** that answers a question you have. Show kids how you look for words similar to the words in your question, then read under the heading to find the information. Be sure to "read" any visual features as well as text.

- Continue to **use the *I Wonder/I Learned* chart** to show how reading often answers our questions. (Start a new chart if using a new text.)

. . . Let's look at this book again (or preview a new text together). In our last session, we used the table of contents to help us. Now, let's explore how we can read with questions in our mind and use *headings* to help us. The headings are like a movie preview: they give us information about what will follow in the section or on the page.

. . . Turn and talk about questions you have that weren't answered when we used the table of contents. (If using a new text, have kids think of questions during the preview and write them on Post-its.)

. . . As you read today, I think you will find the headings really helpful. Let me show you how they work. (Model with a question you have when you see the first heading. Read and think aloud so students see how helpful the headings are in navigating text.)

. . . We'll use the *I Wonder/I Learned* chart again to keep track of our questions and the answers we find. (Model with your question and answer. If using a new text, have kids start a new chart with their Post-its.)

Guide/Support Practice

TEACHING MOVES

- **Have kids read and use their charts** to keep track of their questions and the answers they find in the text.

- **Guide and support** students as needed.

TEACHING LANGUAGE

. . . Now it's your turn to read. Keep track of your questions on your *I Wonder/I Learned* chart.

. . . Remember to use the headings to help you find information in the text.

. . . I will be around to listen and help.

Wrap Up

TEACHING MOVES

- **Have students review** their charts and talk about how the headings helped them. Reinforce that our questions create an authentic purpose for reading. When authors include helpful features, such as a table of contents or headings, we can use them to help us find and learn new information efficiently.

- **If students have lingering questions,** encourage them to explore other texts.

TEACHING LANGUAGE

. . . Let's take a look at our charts. Turn and talk about using headings. How did they help you?

. . . Good job! You've learned something really important in these last two sessions. Good readers work smartly! Using the table of contents and headings often helps us find answers to our questions with ease.

. . . Some of you may have unanswered questions, but don't worry! You can explore them in other books now with these new tools in hand!

ASSESS AND PLAN

Were students able to use their questions and the navigational features to find answers?

Some students may need extra support. Continue modeling and demonstrating how to use various navigational features to support students in learning to gain information and make meaning from features. You may need to confer with some students individually. Keep a basket of books of different levels available for kids to continue to explore on their own.

Reading Conference
Ask Questions

After this unit, you want to know that students are asking and answering questions as they read. The conference focuses on questions students ask about what they are learning and strategies for finding the answers to those questions.

1. **Invite the student to choose a passage to read aloud. Explain that you will expect him or her to stop and ask a question about the text while reading.**
   - Choose a part of your text and read it to me.
   - Tell me what this is about.
   - *(If the student doesn't stop and question on his or her own)* What question(s) do you have about what you are reading right now? What are you wondering?

2. **Focus on what the student wondered while reading.**
   - Did you learn anything new? What do you wonder about that new information?
   - Share some of the questions you were wondering about as you read this.

3. **Ask the student to share a question about the text and continue reading to try to answer it.**
   - What question(s) do you have about this topic (or text) right now?
   - What are some ways you could find the answer(s)? *(Read on. Use the pictures. Talk with others. Use headings. Use a table of contents.)*

Reading Conference Recording Form: Ask Questions

Name _____ Date _____

Book title _____

GOAL	EVIDENCE
The student . . .	This student . . .
1. Understands and questions the text • Tells what the text is about and asks questions about it	
2. Asks questions about new learning • Stops to ask a question to express curiosity about new learning	
3. Reads with a question in mind and uses strategies to answer it • To find answers: – reads on – uses pictures – uses text features • Recognizes that not all questions are answered	

©2010 by Stephanie Harvey, Anne Goudvis, and Judy Wallis. From *Comprehension Intervention: Small-Group Lessons for The Primary Comprehension Toolkit*. Portsmouth, NH: Heinemann. This page may be copied for classroom use only.

Conference Recording Form for "Ask Questions," located in "Resources" section.

- *(After reading on)* Did you find the answer to your question(s)? How?
- Tell me about your lingering questions. What might you do to answer them?

Language students may use to demonstrate that they are asking questions

- I wonder . . .
- Why . . . ?
- How come . . . ?
- What . . . ? Where . . . ? When . . . ? Why . . . ?
- Huh? What's going on here?
- I'm still wondering . . .

Follow-Ups

If the student has difficulty with any of the primary goals in this unit, prompts like the following may be helpful during independent work in subsequent units.

- What did you wonder about as you read?
- Did you remember to stop and ask questions?
- Did you find an answer to your question?
- Did you keep your question in mind as you read?
- Do you have some strategies to get your questions answered?
- Were you ever confused? How did you fix that?

Infer and Visualize

Inferring is the bedrock of understanding. It involves taking what you know, your background knowledge, and merging it with the clues in the text to come up with some information that isn't explicitly stated. Inferential thinking helps readers figure out unfamiliar words, draw conclusions, develop interpretations, make predictions, surface themes, and even create mental images.

Visualizing is sort of a first cousin to inferring. When readers visualize, they construct meaning by creating mental images: seeing, hearing, tasting, touching, and even smelling! Young children seem particularly inclined to visualize in support of understanding as they listen to and read books, often imagining themselves in the text or living in the stories. When children infer and visualize as they listen, read, and view, they respond with joy, glee, or sometimes dread. Inferring and visualizing enable kids to get at the deeper meaning in the text.

> *Inferring involves a willingness to enter into a partnership with an author.* (Wallis, 2005)

Infer with Background Knowledge and Text Clues

In *The Primary Comprehension Toolkit* Lesson 12, students learn about inferring by responding to a read-aloud poem and recording what they infer on thinksheets. The two companion sessions for Lesson 12 offer students more opportunities to infer meaning as they read. In this session, students review what *inferring* means and use Post-its to mark places in the text where they make inferences.

Companion to . . .

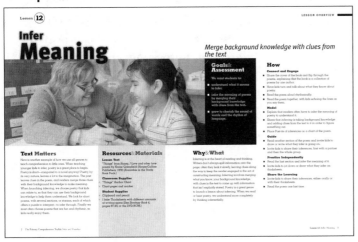

The Primary Comprehension Toolkit
Lesson 12: Infer Meaning

TEXT MATTERS

Inferring offers readers an opportunity to merge their background knowledge with clues left by the author. Some call inferring "gap filling." Select a text that will invite kids to infer—to enter into a partnership with the author. We want kids to draw conclusions, make predictions, dig for themes and ideas, and create images.

Any text that offers some ambiguity will work. "Meet Eric Carle" in *Keep Reading* and "The World Is an Open Book" in *Toolkit Texts: Grades 2–3* invite kids to make inferences. *Bigmama's* by Donald Crews and *When I Was Young in the Mountains* and *Night in the Country* by Cynthia Rylant are good book choices.

SESSION GOALS

We want students to:

- understand what it means to infer.
- infer meaning by merging their background knowledge with clues from the text.

CONSIDERATIONS FOR PLANNING

Inferring is an essential part of reading. Rarely do we read or view something without having to bring our own background knowledge to fill in gaps left by the author. Because the term *inferring* describes a "collection" of actions a reader must take, we help kids see how inferring works through modeling our own thinking.

Students will need Post-its for this session.

Build Background, Word and Concept Knowledge

- **Introduce the term** *inferring*.

- **Offer some real-life examples** to help kids see how much inferring is part of our everyday life.

- **Preview important words** and concepts, using the context to support the meaning.

. . . Today we are going to learn about something very important for readers.

. . . How many of you have been reading or listening to a story being read, and you realize that you are a little confused—you lack some of the information you need, and there's a gap you need to fill? That happens to all of us, doesn't it?

. . . When we fill that gap from our own background knowledge and experience, we call it *inferring*. To infer is to work with the author so that we understand. Sometimes the author gives us a lot of information to use, and other times we must work a little harder.

. . . A few words or ideas may be new to you when we read today. Here's one . . . .

Teach/Model

- **Show students the cover** (or title of the article). Think aloud as you infer, or predict, what the text will be about.

- **Read and model the inferring process.** Help students see that inferring involves merging background knowledge and text clues:

    My background knowledge and experiences + text clues = an inference.

- **Show kids how you record inferences** on Post-its and code them.

- **Spend sufficient time modeling** to ensure students' success during guided practice and when they read independently.

. . . We are going to explore how we infer to help us better understand what we read.

. . . This book (article) will give us lots of opportunities to team up with the author by using our own background knowledge and experiences.

. . . Let's look at the cover. Listen as I infer, or predict, what I think this book will be about.

. . . Now listen as I read and think about the meaning. (Provide a model by reading several pages, or a section of the article, and sharing how you merge your background knowledge and experiences with clues from the text. Clues may be words, actions, events, and pictures in the text.)

. . . When I make an inference, I am going to write my inference on a Post-it and place it right in the text at the spot where I inferred. Watch me write. I will code my thinking with an *I* for *infer.* (Demonstrate how you write and/or draw and label on a Post-it to record your inference. Code the Post-it with an *I*.)

. . . Turn and talk about what you saw me doing.

. . . Would someone like to share what you observed me doing? Great! You are so right. You saw me pause when I was reading and think about this part . . . . When that happened, I used my background knowledge and experience to help me infer the meaning. And I recorded my inference and coded it with an *I* on a Post-it!

Guide/Support Practice

- **Have students read and infer.** Remind them to write or draw their inferences on Post-its.

- Move among the students, listening in on their reading and inferring. **Offer support as necessary.**

. . . Now it's your turn. I'll give you some Post-its. You can write or draw your inferences as you read.

. . . I will come around to hear you read and to help you with your inferring.

Wrap Up

- **Review what students did.** Debriefing is critical. It offers a time for students to share any observations they made about inferring. It also offers insights that help in planning further instructional steps.

- **Invite students to share** some of their Post-its and inferences.

. . . So, what did you notice as you read? Right! You found some places where you had to really think about the words, actions, or events in the text. Then you used your own background knowledge and experience to help you understand what was going on.

. . . Let's share a few examples. Look back in your book for places you put a Post-it. Turn and talk with your neighbor, sharing your inferences.

ASSESS AND PLAN

Inferring is complex. What came easily, and what seemed challenging for students?

If certain types of inferences were more challenging, continue modeling. You can demonstrate how you infer from a picture or illustration, or how you understand characters better by inferring about their actions or what they say. As you model, keep a record of the kinds of inferences you make so kids see that inferring is an "umbrella" term for many things we do as readers.

[Students] have to be taught how to read between the lines—to uncover the deeper meaning they might initially gloss over. (Gallagher, 2004)

Infer with Emotions and Senses

This session builds on the previous one, using another text. Students use their emotions and senses along with their background knowledge and clues in the text to infer.

Companion to . . .

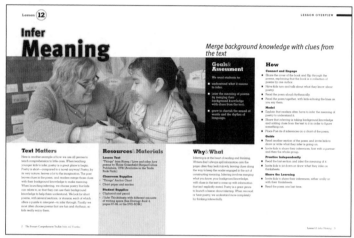

The Primary Comprehension Toolkit
Lesson 12: Infer Meaning

TEXT MATTERS

We want to select a text that requires kids to infer by drawing upon their emotions and senses. Realistic fiction is a good choice because the stories draw from real life.

Stories such as *The Other Side* by Jacqueline Woodson, *A Chair for My Mother* by Vera Williams, and *Saturday Market* by Patricia Grossman engage kids' emotions and senses. If you use a story, it should be new to your students.

A short text also works well. "Let's Go Hiking!" in *Keep Reading* and "My Puppy Is Born" and "Shadows" in *Toolkit Texts: Grades 2–3* offer opportunities for kids to draw on their own experiences, emotions, and senses to make inferences.

CONSIDERATIONS FOR PLANNING

Often students believe that the meaning lies in the text. We want them to see that their thinking matters more than anything. This session further engages kids in seeing how they draw from their own knowledge and experiences to make meaning as they read.

When kids infer, they often relate to the people and the events in the text. This connection is critical because it activates and engages their own emotions and experiences, deepening their understanding.

Students will need Post-its for this session.

SESSION GOALS

We want students to:

- understand what it means to infer.
- infer by merging their background knowledge with clues from the text.
- infer by using emotions and senses.

Build Background, Word and Concept Knowledge

TEACHING MOVES

- **Review the term** *inferring* and the inferring equation: *My background knowledge and experiences + clues from the text = an inference.*

- Introduce the idea that we **use our emotions and senses** as we read. Often something in a text will remind us of personal experience we have that enhances our understanding of the text. Along with the experience, we recall sensory details and emotions associated with the experience.

TEACHING LANGUAGE

. . . The last time we met, we talked about something very important to readers and reading. Anyone remember?

. . . Right! We talked about inferring! We made a little equation, like in math. What was that?

> *My background knowledge and experiences + clues from the text = an inference.*

. . . Today we will explore how we depend on our emotions and senses when we infer. What are our five senses? That's right: seeing, hearing, touching, tasting, and smelling. When we connect something we read to our own experience, we can use our emotions and senses to make inferences.

Teach/Model

- **Engage kids in previewing** the text and anticipating the content. Interesting, provocative introductions get readers' "inference juices" flowing. Talk about any vocabulary that may be unfamiliar.

- Explain that a *prediction* **is a special kind of inference:** we infer and think ahead about what's going to happen in the story. Kids make reasonable predictions when they tie these directly to the text. (See *The Primary Toolkit* Strategy Book 4: *Infer and Visualize* Lesson 15 for additional information.)

. . . I selected a book I think you will like. (Briefly introduce the book and why you think kids will enjoy it, without offering too much information. Preview pertinent vocabulary.)

. . . Let's look at the cover and predict what this text will be about. A *prediction* is a special kind of inference: we infer and think ahead about what's going to happen in the story. What predictions do you have based on the title, the illustration, and what I've just told you? Remember to link your predictions to what you notice on the cover.

. . . Wow! I heard someone make a connection between this text and her own experience. That is exactly what we do when we infer! We think about the words and events in the text based on our own experiences.

. . . I'm going to read and think aloud for you, to show you how we use both our background knowledge and experiences *and* the feelings and emotions that go with those experiences. Our feelings and emotions help us make inferences from the text. (Demonstrate how you keep track of your inferences on a Post-it.)

. . . Turn and talk about what you saw me doing.

. . . Great thinking! Yes, I think about my own experiences *when* the experience relates to the text and situations in the story. I recall my own experiences, and that causes me to infer about what is happening in the text.

Guide/Support Practice

- **Have students read and infer.** Remind them to write or draw their inferences on Post-its and code them.

- Move among the students, listening in on their reading and inferring. **Offer support as necessary.**

. . . Now it's your turn. I will come around to hear you read and to help you with your own inferring. Remember to leave footprints of your thinking by using Post-its. Draw or write your inferences on Post-its and code them with *I*.

Wrap Up

- **Review what kids did.** Make sure kids understand that they draw on their experiences and associated feelings and emotions to fill gaps the author has left in the text. Inferring is a bit like completing a puzzle; the author and the reader each do their part to create the complete picture.

- Have students **share their inferences.** Listen in as the students turn and talk with one another, making sure the inferences they share have sufficient support in the text.

. . . What did you notice as you read? (Prompt students to notice that we use our own experiences to recall feelings and emotions that help us respond to the text.)

. . . Share some examples from your reading. Look back in your book for places you put a Post-it. Turn and talk.

. . . Good thinking!

ASSESS AND PLAN

Consider the quality of the inferences students made. Did they "fill the gaps" left by the author so that their inferences deepened their understanding of the text?

Inferring requires kids to connect to their experiences. Just as we caution kids that not all connections are helpful, we help them analyze their inferences. We want kids to see that inferring fills gaps left by the author. If students' inferences did not deepen their understanding, model and guide them to check clues in the text and revise their inferences. You may want to confer with kids individually to help them analyze their inferences.

When I describe the process of visualizing . . . , I tell students, 'Visualizing is like making my own movie, and the screen is my mind.'
(Robb, 2000)

Infer and Visualize with Poetry

In *The Primary Comprehension Toolkit* Lesson 13, students learn to infer and visualize with poetry. They turn and talk, act out the poem, and draw what they visualize. This companion session for Lesson 13 offers students more time and support for visualizing with poetry. Kids review the terms *inferring* and *visualizing* and then practice with two poems, one they annotate with the teacher and one they read and annotate independently.

Companion to . . .

The Primary Comprehension Toolkit
Lesson 13: Learn to Visualize

Text Matters

We want to select poems that have "holes" for kids to fill. Texts that offer kids opportunities to connect to their own experiences are necessary if we want them to visualize. We must provide texts kids can relate to so their own experiences will help them in their understanding.

The poem "Fireflies" in *Toolkit Texts: Grades 2–3* works well. We also recommend poems from the collection *Honey, I Love* by Eloise Greenfield, a *Toolkit* trade book. You might also use poems from *Keep Reading*, which includes "Sensing the Seasons," "My Neighborhood," and "I Like Art!"

Session Goals

We want students to:
- create a picture in their mind as they listen and read.
- understand what it means to visualize and infer with poetry.

Considerations for Planning

Visualizing is a part of inferring. When we infer, we visualize by creating mental and sensory images. These make the text come alive so that our reading is richer. We support the inferences we make by the immediate "pictures" that pop into our heads. Visualizing allows readers to draw upon their images and all the sensory information that surrounds those images and experiences. Visualizing enhances reading, and readers who create images find reading more enjoyable and engaging.

Write the poem you have chosen for modeling and guided reading on chart paper. Provide the same poem on plain paper for kids.

Provide an additional poem on plain paper for kids to read independently.

Build Background, Word and Concept Knowledge

TEACHING MOVES

- **Review the inferring equation:** *My background knowledge and experiences + clues from the text = an inference.*

- Explain that **when we infer, we often *visualize,*** or "see" what the author includes in the text, by using images from our own experience. Our experiences aren't exactly the same, but we begin with what we know and connect that to the author's words and ideas.

TEACHING LANGUAGE

. . . When we last met, we talked about inferring as filling in gaps. Who can recall the equation we made? That's right! *My background knowledge and experiences + clues from the text = an inference.*

. . . When we infer, we often visualize something happening, too. *Visualizing* is "seeing" in our mind what the author is telling us in the text.

. . . For example, when I say, "I hear thunder rumbling," how many of you see storm clouds in your mind and smell the rain in the air? Turn and talk about what you "see" in your mind, or what you smell, hear, or feel in your mind when I say, "I hear thunder rumbling."

Teach/Model

TEACHING MOVES

- Explain that when we visualize, **we call on our senses** to support our understanding.

- Write a poem on a chart. Read it through to kids first. Then go back to the beginning and **model how you visualize and infer.**

- **Note what you infer and visualize** next to the poem. Invite kids to share and record what they visualize on their copies of the poem.

- **Have kids practice** inferring and visualizing with the same poem. Then they can try it on their own with other poems.

Teaching Tip

Visualizing becomes more and more critical for readers as they mature. Make a habit of stopping to talk about what kids "see" in their heads as you read throughout the day. The more opportunities they have to think and talk about what they visualize, the more easily the habit of visualizing will be formed.

TEACHING LANGUAGE

. . . I'm going to show you how visualizing works with a poem. When I read a poem, I visualize "pictures" in my mind. I pay attention to the poem's words, but I create my image using the words and my own experiences.

. . . I'm going to read the poem all the way through to enjoy it first.

. . . When I read these words . . . , I got a picture in my mind. I'm going to sketch it right here next to the poem.

. . . And when I read these words . . . , I was inferring. I thought . . . . I'll jot my thoughts right next to the poem, too. And I used my other senses . . . (Share what you smelled, heard, felt—whatever senses are prompted by the poem.)

. . . Let's keep reading together. Let's find places in the text where you visualized what was happening. Sketch or jot your thoughts right next to the poem.

. . . One more thought I want to share with you: Visualizing is like making a movie in our minds. It makes reading much more enjoyable!

Guide/Support Practice

- **Give students the new poem.** As you listen to individual kids read, ask them to share with you the visual images they are forming in their minds.

> **Teaching Tip**
> Some kids will need nudging. They may be visualizing without realizing it. The teacher's nudging will help students pay attention to and use their own images to enrich their understanding.

. . . Your turn now! Here is a new poem for you to read. Continue visualizing and inferring, and I will be around to listen in.

. . . Be sure to sketch your images and write your inferences next to your poem.

Wrap Up

- **Help kids look back** through the poem to find and share places they visualized.

- **Help kids understand** that we create different pictures, or images, in our minds because our individual experiences are different.

. . . Who has an image to share? Super! Tell us the words from the poem, and share what you saw in your mind or inferred as you read.

. . . Not all our images are exactly the same. We all have different background knowledge we use to create our images. But because you used the poet's words and ideas and connected them to your own, each one of your images helped you better understand the text.

. . . This is very cool, isn't it?

. . . So, visualizing is when . . . . Help me finish that sentence!

ASSESS AND PLAN

Look over the poems students have annotated. Does their visualizing and inferring reflect understanding of the text?

Through conferring, make sure kids have used text references and visual images to understand the poem's meaning. You might want to share out their ideas about their individual poem's meaning.

Are some students still having difficulty visualizing?

Some readers either make fewer images or are less aware of images they make. Sometimes kids can "act out" a phrase or line of a poem to help create pictures in their own or other students' minds. Plan time to confer with those students. Fill a basket with a variety of texts that invite visualizing, and let kids know they are available. Use read-aloud time to offer additional models of your own visualizing and inferring, and invite discussion by having kids turn and talk.

By teaching our children to
read, think, and talk about
their thinking, we enable
them not only to have
purposeful conversations
that construct meaning
with others, but also to have
raging conversations in their
own heads. (Nichols, 2006)

Companion to . . .

The Primary Comprehension Toolkit
Lesson 14: Make Sense of New
Information

Infer and Visualize with Nonfiction

In *The Primary Comprehension Toolkit* Lesson 14, students learn how to infer and visualize with nonfiction text. This companion session for Lesson 14 offers students more time and support for inferring and visualizing with nonfiction. They focus on using clues in the text, both words and features, to support their inferences.

TEXT MATTERS

Select a text with features that lend themselves to inferring and visualizing, such as a book from the *Creepy Creatures* series. More challenging texts include *Spiders* by Ann O. Squire and *My Best Book of Sharks* by Claire Llewellyn.

A short article such as "Symmetry in Nature" from *Keep Reading* has enough information and clues in the text and features to support kids in inferring and visualizing.

SESSION GOALS

We want students to:

- learn the language of inferring and visualizing and use it to describe their inner conversation.
- combine their background knowledge with clues from the text to make reasonable inferences.
- talk about, draw, and record what they infer and visualize to facilitate learning from informational text.

CONSIDERATIONS FOR PLANNING

Readers use their background knowledge and experience to infer and visualize. When kids read narrative texts, inferring and visualizing seem to come a bit more naturally. As humans, we organize our lives around stories. So, when kids read stories, they tend to have a ready storehouse of experience they can use to make inferences about the characters and events of the story.

When kids read informational texts, they need to pay close attention to the text clues—the pictures, text features, vocabulary, and information. They need to tie their experiences to the text, not make wild guesses, to better understand what they read.

Build Background, Word and Concept Knowledge

TEACHING MOVES

- **Review the inference equation:** *Text clues + background knowledge = an inference.* We want kids to keep this equation in mind as they make inferences in informational texts.

- **Review the language** of inferring: *I think* or *I infer.*

- Remind kids of the importance of **being able to point to clues** in the text to support their inferences.

- **Quickly review** text and visual features.

- **Preview any vocabulary** that will support kids to better understand the text.

TEACHING LANGUAGE

. . . Remember, we have been talking a lot about how we become partners with the author when we infer. Let's write the equation to show what happens when we infer. (Write the following equation.)

Text clues + background knowledge = an inference

. . . When we infer, we might say *I think* or *I infer* to signal others that we are using clues from the text *and* our background knowledge.

. . . We infer when we read stories and poems. We also infer when we read nonfiction. Inferring in nonfiction is very important. But it is super important *not* to make wild guesses. We always want to be able to point to clues in the text to support what we infer.

. . . We will be using the text features and visual features, too. Who can remember some we have talked about?

. . . Some words may be new to you as we read today. Here's one . . .

Teach/Model

- **Preview the text together.** Helping kids use the language of reading is important. When we teach kids strategies, we are really teaching them a series of moves they make to accomplish a specific purpose. By using precise and consistent language such as *I infer* or *I think* or *I visualize*, we help kids recall the strategic moves we make as we model.

- **Model how you read** and use the features as well as the text to infer and visualize. Since inferring often includes using context clues to unlock the meaning of unknown words, look for a way to model that for students.

- Show how you **write and sketch on a Post-it** to record what you infer and visualize. Code the Post-it and leave it beside the clues in the text.

. . . I have a great book (or article) for us to read. It is so interesting! It is a nonfiction book about . . .

. . . Let's look at the cover and the title. As you look at the cover, turn and talk about something you infer. Use reader language like *I infer* or *I think* as you share.

. . . Good thinking!

. . . Let's look on in the text now. I'm going to read a bit and show you how I use my background knowledge and the text clues—the words, information, and features—when I read. Watch how I use the words *I infer, I visualize,* and *I think* when I combine my background knowledge with the clues in the text. I can also sketch a mind picture I create based on the text—remember, that's inferring, too! (Read part of the text and think aloud as you infer and visualize.)

. . . Turn and talk about what you saw me doing.

. . . I am going to write one of our inferences and sketch an image on a Post-it and place it where we inferred in the text. I will code the Post-it with an *I* to show I inferred and a *V* to show I visualized. (Use either your own inference or a student's inference to model.)

Guide/Support Practice

- **Do at least one example together.** Remind kids they will use both the features and the words to infer, along with their own background knowledge.

- **Have kids read on,** recording on Post-its what they infer and visualize. Remind them to infer the meaning of unfamiliar words.

- Move among the students to listen in and **offer support as needed.**

> **Teaching Tip**
>
> Be sure to note how kids are navigating the pages of text. This is one of the most difficult aspects of nonfiction. Kids often read only the connected text and forget they can gain valuable information from the visual and text features.

. . . Now I want you to try it. We will do a page (or section) together. Let's see how it works. (Read the page or section of text, stopping and inviting kids to offer their inferences.)

. . . Now you read on. Be sure to draw or write your inferences on Post-its.

. . . If you come to an unfamiliar word, jot down or draw what you think it means.

. . . Keep reading. I will be around to listen in.

Wrap Up

- **Help students share** and "unpack" their inferences by asking about the clues they used.

. . . Good work today! Let's talk about some of the inferences you made. Include the big question: What clues helped you infer and visualize?

. . . Talking about how the text clues help us is really important. Quickly turn and talk about an inference you made, and tell how the text clues helped you infer.

ASSESS AND PLAN

Did students use the language of inferring with ease?

Noticing and naming is important. When kids are able to use language to name what they do, that knowledge "belongs" to them. If kids are still having trouble, reread a page or section of the text with them and make a chart to record information that is stated in the text and information they infer or visualize.

"
To infer as we read is to go
beyond the literal interpre-
tation and to open a world
of meaning connected to our
lives. (Keene and Zimmer-
mann, 1997)
"

Companion to . . .

The Primary Comprehension Toolkit
Lesson 15: Infer and Visualize with
Narrative Nonfiction

Infer with Narrative Nonfiction

In *The Primary Comprehension Toolkit* Lesson 15, kids infer and visualize during a read-aloud with a narrative nonfiction picture book. They make an *I Learned/I Inferred* chart and consider big ideas and lingering questions. This companion session offers students the opportunity to practice inferring with another narrative nonfiction story. This session is an important one and has lots for kids to learn. It may span two days.

Text Matters

Narrative nonfiction texts that leave some "holes" for the reader to fill are perfect for this session. Books like *Working Cotton* by Sherley Anne Williams and *Bread Comes to Life* by George Levenson invite readers to infer and visualize as they learn information from the text and pictures .

Short texts such as "Don't Trash the Earth" from *Keep Reading* and "Sam Goes Trucking" and "Rock Secrets" from *Toolkit Texts: Grades 2–3* include both words and pictures so the reader has an opportunity to use both as sources of information.

Considerations for Planning

It is important to help kids see how they merge their background knowledge and what the author provides to make sense of a text. Sometimes kids understand small details without understanding the big ideas. For example, in *Working Cotton*, they might understand that the cotton sack is large and heavy without understanding how difficult it would be to work an entire day carrying the sack. We want to help kids see that, as we read, we infer small details *and* link those details to the larger ideas.

In narrative nonfiction, we want kids to follow the plotline or sequence as well as use the information they encounter to infer and visualize.

Students will need Post-its for this session.

Session Goals

We want students to:

- combine their background knowledge with text and picture clues to draw inferences, make predictions, and visualize with narrative nonfiction.

- draw inferences and create mind pictures in response to information, unfamiliar vocabulary, and the story.

- infer big ideas and consider lingering questions prompted by the text.

Build Background, Word and Concept Knowledge

- **Review the inference equation:** *Text clues + background knowledge = inference.*

- Explain that the text's illustrations "carry" some of the meaning. Remind kids to **use clues from both the text and pictures** as they learn and infer.

- Remind students they can use the inferring equation to **figure out unfamiliar words.**

. . . Who can coach me as I write the inference equation? (Have kids help in creating the equation.)

> *Text clues + background knowledge = inference*

. . . We are going to read a special kind of text today. It will give us information, *and* it will tell a story. We call these texts narrative (story) non-fiction (information). This text also has pictures that help to tell the story and give information.

. . . When we read a text like this, we have to keep up with the events in the story as well as the information we are learning. Our own experiences help us infer and visualize. That is a lot to work on!

. . . Remember, we can use our inferring equation to figure out unfamiliar words.

Teach/Model

- **Preview the text together.** Narrative text structure is familiar to kids, but they are less used to information being presented that way. Reading to follow the story and reading to learn each present challenges. When kids must do both, we need to help them find ways to follow the sequence of events, or storyline, while also paying attention to the new information they are encountering.

- Model how to **use more reader's language.** In addition to *I infer* and *I think*, kids will use *I learned* in this session.

- **Introduce the chart.** While kids will simultaneously track events in the story and their learning, focus their attention on the chart. After kids have read, you can review and discuss the storyline so kids see how the author used the story to provide information.

- **Show kids how to record on Post-its.** Model how to code the Post-its: *L* for *learned* and *I* for *inferred.* Place your Post-its on the chart so kids see how they will use their Post-its at the end of the session.

- **Preview unfamiliar words.** Show students how they can use context to infer the meaning of a new word.

. . . Let's look at the story I've brought. As you look at the cover (or first page of an article), what can you infer about the content? (Invite kids to use clues on the cover to predict content.)

. . . What do you know about . . . that you might use to help you as you read today? Great! Those are all things that will help you as you read.

. . . Let's look at the text. Because it is a story, we know we have to keep track of the events as they unfold. We'll also keep track of what we are learning.

. . . Let's see how this works. I'll read the first page (or part of a short text).

. . . I learned that . . . That makes me infer that . . . . (Use Post-its to keep track, since we will ask kids to do that in their texts. Code the Post-its with *L* for *learned, I* for *inferred.*)

. . . Turn and talk about what you are thinking. Remember to use reader's language: *I infer* or *I think.* Let's add one more phrase, *I learned*, because you will be learning from this story, too!

. . . Let's make a chart to record what we learn and what we infer. Watch how I use Post-its to record what I learned from the first page and what I inferred. (Write or draw on the Post-its and place them on the chart.)

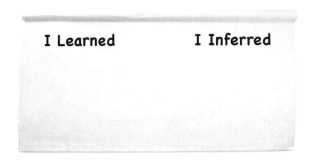

I Learned	I Inferred

. . . Let's read another page together so you see how this works.

Guide/Support Practice

- **Have students read,** using Post-its to record and code what they learn and infer.

- **Coach as necessary** as you listen to individual students. Make sure kids understand that new learning *becomes* new background knowledge from which they can infer.

- **If the story is too long** to finish in one session, tell kids where to stop reading.

. . . Time for you to try it now. Use your Post-its to keep track of what you are learning and what you are inferring.

. . . I will be around to listen and help!

Wrap Up

TEACHING MOVES

- **Have students share** what they learned and inferred. Add their ideas to the chart.

- This session **may span two days** because it is so rich with learning opportunities.

- **On the first day,** have kids select Post-its to add to the group chart. Help them connect *I learned* and *I inferred* Post-its. If kids didn't infer from some of the new learning, prompt for what they might infer, and add to the chart.

- **The next day,** help students review the story and use what they learned and inferred to think about the big ideas. Invite them to share any lingering questions.

TEACHING LANGUAGE

Day 1

. . . Take a minute to turn and talk about what you learned and what you inferred.

. . . Let's see what we can add to our chart.

. . . Great thinking today! Tomorrow we will continue thinking about this story. Now that we understand what happened, we'll be thinking more about the big ideas in the story.

Day 2

. . . Let's review the story. (Review the storyline. If kids didn't complete the story, have them finish reading.)

. . . Now let's look back at our *I Learned/I Inferred* chart. Let's see how the author used the story to help us learn more about . . . Let's review the inferences we made as we read . . . .

. . . Great thinking! So, one big idea we inferred from reading this story is . . . And another is . . .

. . . Some of you may still wonder about some things in the story. When we don't have enough clues to infer, we are left with lingering questions to research! Does anyone have a lingering question?

ASSESS AND PLAN

Did students use the story structure to notice what they learned and then to infer using the author's clues?

Some kids will need more modeling. Helping kids see that they combine their background knowledge with the text and picture clues to infer, predict, and visualize—both to keep track of the storyline and to learn information—is complex. Consider charting storylines in read-alouds so kids become more aware of text structure.

What kinds of inferences did students make in response to the information presented in the text?

If students missed opportunities to use the information in the text to infer, consider using another narrative nonfiction text to offer additional modeling and practice.

Reading Conference

Infer and Visualize

After this unit, you want to know that students make inferences and create visual images to better understand what they are reading, so your conference should help the student talk about how she or he infers and visualizes while reading.

1. **Invite the reader to choose a passage and create a context for it.**
   - Choose a part of your book to read to me.
   - Tell me what you were inferring and/or visualizing as you read that part.
   - *(If the student doesn't stop to make inferences or describe visual images on his or her own)* What are you visualizing? What inferences are you making as you read?

2. *(If the student is reading fiction or poetry)* **Focus on the inferences and visual images the reader created as she or he read.**
   - Share some of the inferences you made as you read.
   - Tell me about the pictures you created in your mind as you read.
   - *(If reading fiction)* What do you think is going to happen next? Make a prediction.

3. *(If the student is reading nonfiction)* **Ask the reader to infer and visualize to make sense of information.**
   - What clues in the text did you combine with your background knowledge to make an inference? What did you infer?
   - *(If the text has features like photographs or subheads)* What can you infer from this feature? What information does it give you?
   - Share a place in the text where you created a picture in your mind. What did you visualize?

Reading Conference Recording Form: Infer and Visualize	
Name _____ Date _____	
Book title _____	
GOAL	**EVIDENCE**
The student . . .	This student . . .
1. Understands the text • Tells what the book is about and talks about what he or she was visualizing and inferring while reading	
2. (If reading fiction or poetry) Is aware of her or his own visualizing and inferring strategies • Describes and explains inferences and mental images that enhance the meaning of the text • Makes inferences to predict what is going to happen next	
3. Infers and visualizes to make sense of information • Combines text clues with background knowledge to understand part of the text • (If reading nonfiction with features) Infers information from features • Visualizes information from the text	

©2010 by Stephanie Harvey, Anne Goudvis, and Judy Wallis. From *Comprehension Intervention: Small-Group Lessons for The Primary Comprehension Toolkit.* Portsmouth, NH: Heinemann. This page may be copied for classroom use only.

Conference Recording Form for "Infer and Visualize," located in "Resources" section.

Follow-Ups

If a student has difficulty with any of the primary goals in this unit, prompts like the following may be helpful during independent work in subsequent units.

- What are you thinking? What are you inferring or visualizing?
- How did you make meaning as you read these words/phrases/sentences?
- How might inferring help you figure out that part of the text?
- Are you creating pictures in your mind that help you understand the text?
- What did you learn as you read this? What inferences did you make as you read this?

Language students may use to demonstrate that they are monitoring meaning

- I infer . . . I think . . . Maybe . . .
- I am creating a picture in my mind right here.
- I combined my background knowledge with text clues to make an inference . . . so I infer . . .
- These words paint a picture in my mind. They make me feel, see, hear . . .
- I think this part means . . .
- I learned . . . and I inferred . . .

Determine Importance

When we read nonfiction, we are reading to learn and remember information. Once kids know how to merge their thinking with text information, it's time to help them figure out what it makes sense to remember. We can't possibly remember every fact or piece of information we read, nor should we. We teach kids to tell the difference between interesting details and salient, important information. When kids learn to paraphrase, they are well on their way to understanding the information and shaping it into their own thought. Kids also learn to distinguish among facts, questions, and responses so they can sort and sift information to better organize it. They use note-taking scaffolds to hold their thinking as they prepare to share it with others.

Determining importance has to do with knowing why you're reading and then making decisions about which information or ideas are most critical to understanding the overall meaning of the piece. (Zimmermann and Hutchins, 2003)

Companion to . . .

The Primary Comprehension Toolkit
Lesson 16: Figure Out What's Important

Identify Important Ideas

In *The Primary Comprehension Toolkit* Lesson 16, students read an article about Helen Keller and make a chart to distinguish important information from interesting details. The two companion sessions for Lesson 16 offer students more support for figuring out what's important. In this session, they identify the big, important ideas in a new text.

TEXT MATTERS

Select a text that has just a few big ideas. Texts with headings related to the big ideas are especially good because headings help readers navigate text to link details to big ideas.

From Seed to Sunflower by Anita Ganeri and *Spiders* by Monica Hughes are well designed. Biographies, such as *The Silent Witness: A True Story of the Civil War* by Robin Friedman, work well for linking details to big ideas. If you use a book, kids can finish it in the next session.

Short texts such as "Postcards from the Desert Museum" in *Keep Reading* and "Slithering Snakes," "Wings in the Water," and "Seeing with Sound" in *Toolkit Texts: Grades 2–3* have features that help kids identify the big ideas.

CONSIDERATIONS FOR PLANNING

All readers are intrigued by interesting details. We help kids distinguish the big, important ideas from those that are simply interesting. Showing kids how to work from small, interesting details to big ideas and also how to work from big ideas to the smaller details helps them see that details cluster around bigger ideas.

In this session, we teach kids how to determine the most important information to enrich their background knowledge.

Students will need Post-its.

SESSION GOALS

We want students to:

- recognize and understand what a detail is.
- distinguish important information from interesting details.
- code important information in the text with a star.

Build Background, Word and Concept Knowledge

- Explain to kids that all readers have to figure out and **keep track of what is important** as they read.

- **Share an authentic story** from your experience to show how easy it is for even adult readers to become distracted. When we share our own experiences, we help kids see that their experiences in trying to remember important details are not unique.

- **Talk about** *skimming* **and** *scanning.* Explain that skimming and scanning before we read helps us get ideas about what is important in the text. Scanning for key ideas helps us organize in advance and cluster information as we read.

- **Preview unfamiliar vocabulary** or concepts to ensure kids will understand the text.

. . . One of the most important things we do as readers is figure out and keep track of what is important. Sometimes things that are interesting to us distract us from thinking about the most important things.

. . . (We suggest you tell your own story here.) Once I was reading a book about the life cycle of a frog. As I read, I kept track of the important information about the different stages. Then the author added this fascinating information about how tadpoles look like leaves so they camouflage themselves. I was so amazed; I had never known that! I had to have an inner conversation about what was important. After all, I was reading to learn about the life cycle of a frog.

. . . One way we can gather the most important information is by skimming and scanning, or looking through the text, before we begin to read. This helps us get a sense of what is most important and how we can "cluster" details around bigger, more important ideas. I'll show you how it works.

. . . Before we read, here are a few words you will need to know . . .

Teach/Model

- **Model skimming and scanning** as you preview the text. Show kids how you glean information about big ideas from the connected text, the pictures, and the text features. Think aloud as you peruse the book or article.

- **Read the first page** (or section). Invite kids to share what they notice.

- **Create an anchor chart** to record interesting details and important information.

> **Teaching Tip**
>
> It is important to tell kids that reading nonfiction is different from reading fiction. We don't skim and scan fiction in the same way. It wouldn't be very helpful to scan a story all the way to the ending! This kind of knowledge is "conditional" knowledge; it helps kids know under what conditions a reader takes certain actions.

. . . Today I want to share this book (article) with you. Like many nonfiction texts, it has lots of small details that make it interesting. It also has some really big, important ideas that I need to remember.

. . . Let's preview by skimming and scanning. Look at this . . . Notice how I use the pictures and visual features as well as the text features to help me get a good sense about the content. This will help me "collect" the small details around the big ideas.

. . . Now I will read the first page (or section).

. . . Turn and talk about what you are noticing.

. . . What smaller ideas did you find interesting but unnecessary to remember? (Have kids explain what they are noticing.) Let's make an anchor chart to show our thinking.

Interesting Details	Important Information

. . . The big ideas are like magnets; they attract the smaller ideas like a magnet attracts paperclips! However, we don't have to remember all details!

Guide/Support Practice

- Show kids how to **draw a star on a Post-it** to code a big idea. Place it near a big idea in the text to demonstrate what you want kids to do.

- **Have students read** part or all of the text, using Post-its to note important ideas and code them with a star as they read. Leave time at the end of the session to add to the chart.

- Move among students to listen in and **offer support as needed.**

. . . You try it now. Instead of using a chart, I'll give you some Post-its. When you see a really important idea, jot it on a Post-it and code it with a star. We use a star to help us keep track of the most important ideas. (Demonstrate how to code an idea with a star.)

. . . Try making a star on one of your Post-its. I will help you, and then you'll have it ready when you find a big idea!

. . . Turn and talk about what you will do as you read.

. . . I will be around to listen to your reading and help as you need me.

Wrap Up

- **Add to the chart.** Invite kids to share big ideas they found as they read. Ask if anyone found an interesting detail.

- Some students will have difficulty sorting ideas. **Support kids in reclassifying** their ideas if necessary.

- **For the next session,** have kids leave their Post-its in the text.

. . . Let's share what we found! Someone start us off. Who wants to share something important you learned in the text? (Add to the chart.)

. . . Did anyone notice an interesting detail that we can add to the chart?

. . . Good thinking! (Be sure to help kids reclassify their information if they selected a detail as an important idea.)

. . . Leave your Post-its in your text. We will look at them again in our next session.

ASSESS AND PLAN

Did some students have difficulty sorting ideas into the two categories?
To demonstrate how smaller details map onto bigger ideas, draw a circle with a big idea in the center. Have kids write interesting details on Post-its and place them around the circle to show that they are interesting details, but the big idea is in the center.

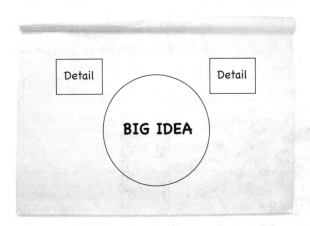

Were students able to code big ideas with a star?
If students had difficulty coding ideas with a star, consider giving them Post-its in two colors: one color for interesting details and another color for big ideas. Seeing the two colors sometimes help students realize there are fewer big ideas.

The challenge to "determine what is important" is also about "determining what is unimportant." This challenge also involves coming to understand how ideas are related to each other and how a text structures and presents ideas.
(Calkins, 2001)

Companion to . . .

The Primary Comprehension Toolkit
Lesson 16: Figure Out What's
Important

Session Goals

We want students to:

- recognize and understand what a detail is.
- distinguish important information from interesting details.
- code important information in the text with a star.

Delete Ideas That Aren't Important

This session picks up where the previous session leaves off. Students look back at the text and consider which Post-its with stars are really big ideas and which can be deleted. Then they continue reading and recording big ideas, either in the same text or in a new text.

Text Matters

Continue with the previous session's text if students didn't complete the reading. If they did, select anther short text to reinforce the concept of big, important ideas and interesting but less important details.

Short texts that will help kids see big ideas in relationship to the details include "Watch Me Grow!" in *Keep Reading* and "Animal Helpers," "Wings in the Water," and "Seeing with Sound" in *Toolkit Texts: Grades 2–3.*

Considerations for Planning

Consider how easily kids distinguished the big, important ideas from those that were simply interesting in the previous session. Determining importance is practicing the "art of deletion!"

You will need the anchor chart from the previous session.

Students will need their text with Post-its from the previous session.

Students will need more Post-its.

Build Background, Word and Concept Knowledge

- **Review what kids did** in the previous session. Check to be sure kids are clear regarding the difference between big, important ideas and interesting but less important details.

- Have kids **revisit the anchor chart** and discuss what they notice about the two columns: interesting details and important information. Have kids turn and talk about their perceptions, and listen in. This will offer insights. Being able to articulate the difference is evidence of understanding.

. . . Let's talk about what we did last time. Which of you wants to start us off?

. . . Right! We talked about BIG ideas and smaller, less important details—though some are pretty interesting, aren't they?

. . . Let's look back at the anchor chart we made to investigate the differences. Turn and talk about what you notice.

Teach/Model

- Invite kids to **review the text and their Post-its** from the previous session. Have them consider the ideas they starred, *keep* the really big ideas, and *delete* any unimportant details.

- **Skim and scan** and identify some big ideas together to get kids started. Continue using the same text, or, if kids finished the previous text, introduce a short text that will extend their learning and offer additional practice.

. . . Let's look back at the text we were reading. Turn and talk about what you notice. Look to be sure all your Post-its with stars are really BIG ideas!

. . . Good thinking. Some of you noticed that a few of the ideas by which you placed Post-its are interesting, but they aren't really important. Talk about how you know that.

. . . Right! You could *delete*, or let go or get rid of, some of the details, but we need to *keep* the big ideas!

. . . Today you will continue reading and noting the big ideas (or read another interesting text). Let me start us out. We will do the very same thing we did before: put a Post-it with a star on the important ideas. Let's skim and scan the text to see if we can identify some of the big ideas.

Guide/Support Practice

- **Have students read.** Remind them to record and star the big ideas on Post-its as they read.

- **Provide coaching as needed.** Start with students you think are less secure to be sure they are reading for important ideas.

. . . It's your turn to read now. Be sure to use a Post-it with a star to help keep track of the most important ideas.

. . . I will be around to listen to your reading and help as you need me.

Wrap Up

- **Invite kids to share** their experience and the big ideas they found as they read.

- **Add to the anchor chart** or start a new one if students read a different text.

- **Listen to students** and note where they placed their Post-its.

. . . Let's share. How did it go today? Did you find it easier to pick out the most important information?

. . . Turn and talk and compare your Post-its.

. . . Let's put some of your ideas on our chart. (Start a new chart if kids read a new text.)

. . . Anyone want to share?

Assess and Plan

Are some students still having difficulty sorting the big ideas from the details?

Continue conferring with kids who are still having difficulty. Provide additional think-aloud models, but be sure to involve students quickly so you can hear their thinking. Shift from modeling to coaching, offering just enough support to ensure success.

Would some kids benefit from trying a different approach to separating important ideas from interesting details?

One way to reinforce the difference is to write big ideas and small ideas on index cards. After reading the text, spread the cards out and have children consider which cards could be "deleted" and which must stay because they are very important. Writing "smaller" details on smaller Post-its and big ideas on larger Post-its serves the same purpose—making this distinction more concrete.

> *There is no way to accurately describe the excitement that fills the room when students are exploring nonfiction.*
> (Allison, 2007)

Paraphrase and Respond to Information

In *The Primary Comprehension Toolkit* Lesson 17, students learn the steps of paraphrasing information. This companion session offers students more time and support to practice paraphrasing. They review the term *paraphrase* and then practice paraphrasing information and responding to it as they read.

Companion to . . .

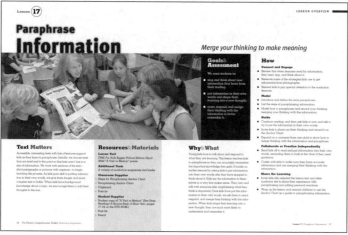

The Primary Comprehension Toolkit
Lesson 17: Paraphrase Information

Text Matters

Select an engaging, accessible text with features that will support kids as they learn to paraphrase. Well-organized books and articles that are relatively short ease readers' first attempts to paraphrase. We want to free kids' thinking energy to focus on the process.

Articles such as "The Grizzly Bear" and "The Bald Eagle" in *Keep Reading* and "Crackle, Flash, Boom" and "From Egg to Salamander" in *Toolkit Texts: Grades 2–3* are well organized and have interesting information for kids to paraphrase and respond to.

Session Goals

We want students to:

- stop and think about new information they learn from their reading.
- put information in their own words and shape their learning into a new thought.
- react, respond, and merge their thinking with the information to better remember it.

Considerations for Planning

Putting information into our own words makes it our own. Understanding is wrapped up in and dependent on our ability to transfer information from an author's text and merge it with our own thinking.

This session builds on previous sessions in which kids began to see the difference between important ideas and details. Now we show students how to paraphrase new learning and merge it with their thinking to enrich their background knowledge.

You will need the anchor charts from the previous sessions.

Students will need Post-its.

Build Background, Word and Concept Knowledge

- **Build on kids' prior learning.** (If possible, display anchor charts from previous sessions.) Have kids turn and talk to review what they have been learning about reading. Explain to kids that all they have been doing—connecting with their own experiences, asking questions, and determining important ideas—will be used in this session.

- **Introduce the term** *paraphrasing*.

> **Teaching Tip**
>
> It's great to keep anchor charts up in the room. They archive prior learning and pull it into the present when we want kids to note it.

. . . Let's talk about all we have been doing. (Just look around at our anchor charts!) Turn and talk about what you have been learning.

. . . Right! We learned to tell the difference between BIG, important ideas and smaller, less important details. We learned how asking great questions during our reading helps us seek answers as we read. We have seen how our background knowledge is so important in inferring and visualizing—and how we are always building more background knowledge as we learn new things.

. . . Today we are going to learn how we can take the words in the texts we read and make them our own. When we do that, we call it *paraphrasing*.

. . . You will continue to use all the good things you have learned and put them to use as we read the text today.

Teach/Model

- **Introduce the text.** Invite kids to turn and talk about the text and the topic. Preview pertinent vocabulary.

- Model how you **read a section and paraphrase** to understand what the text says. Have kids follow along in the text as you demonstrate how to paraphrase. Model what you're thinking as you make the author's ideas your own.

- **Create an anchor chart** to record the steps for paraphrasing. This will help students later. When kids help in the creation of a chart that records group learning, they are more likely to consult it in their independent reading.

- **Create another anchor chart** for examples. Show kids how you identify important information, paraphrase, and respond.

Words/Pictures from the Text	Information in My Own Words
(record information directly from the text, pictures, and other features)	(paraphrase the ideas, adding your own response to show your reaction)

. . . Let's look at this text. What do you notice? There are some words you need to know . . .

. . . I'll read a section. (Be sure to "read" pictures, captions, and any other features.)

. . . Here's an interesting idea. (Select several sentences you can paraphrase.) Listen as I think about this part. I am going to paraphrase it like this, in my own words . . . .

. . . Help me think about what I have just done. I'll write the steps on a chart to help us remember.

Steps for Paraphrasing Information

1. Read the information.
2. Say the information in my own words.
3. React and respond to the information.

. . . I'll make another chart to show how I take the author's words and put them into my own words.

. . . After I paraphrase, I write my reaction to show how I merge the author's ideas with my own background knowledge.

. . . Turn and talk about how paraphrasing works.

. . . Great thinking! Explain why paraphrasing is important. Right! It helps us make the author's ideas our own because when we paraphrase, we have to *actually* understand! We add that information to our own background knowledge.

Guide/Support Practice

TEACHING MOVES

- **Do a section together.** Have kids paraphrase on Post-its. They can add their ideas to the chart later.

- **Have kids continue** reading and paraphrasing on Post-its.

- **Provide coaching as needed.** By now, kids should see that the use of Post-its is flexible and can help capture thinking in a variety of ways. Some students may need to have additional modeling each time the purpose of the Post-its changes.

TEACHING LANGUAGE

. . . Let's read a section together before you read on your own. Instead of the chart, you will use Post-its to record your paraphrases. We will add to our chart when we come back together.

. . . Now it's your turn. Continue to read and paraphrase the big ideas on your Post-its.

. . . I will be around to listen in and help as you need me.

Wrap Up

TEACHING MOVES

- **Invite kids to review** what they did. Refer to the anchor chart of steps for paraphrasing.

- **Add ideas to the chart** of important information and paraphrases. Have kids locate important ideas in the text and read their Post-it paraphrases.

- **Note how kids select ideas** to paraphrase and how they incorporate other strategies. We should hear kids using "reader words" we have taught them.

TEACHING LANGUAGE

. . . How did it go? (Invite kids who met with success to share, and support them in describing what they did. Use the chart of steps for paraphrasing as a scaffold.)

. . . Now let's add to our anchor chart of important ideas from the text and your paraphrases.

. . . Good job!

ASSESS AND PLAN

Were students' paraphrases *really* paraphrases?

If kids had trouble using their own words, give them another model and some short texts they can work on independently. When kids complete them using Post-its to record their paraphrases and thinking, confer with individuals to note understanding.

> *In thoughtful classrooms, a disposition toward thinking is always on display. Teachers show their own curiosity and interest.* (Ritchhart, 2002)

Sort Information, Questions, and Reactions

In *The Primary Comprehension Toolkit* Lesson 18, students record information, questions, and reactions during a read-aloud and sort their notes on an *I Learned/I Wonder/Wow* anchor chart. The two companion sessions for Lesson 18 offer kids an opportunity to practice organizing their thinking as they read a text at their independent level. In this session, they take notes on Post-its and sort them on an *I Learned/I Wonder/Wow* thinksheet.

Companion to . . .

The Primary Comprehension Toolkit
Lesson 18: Organize Your Thinking
as You Read

TEXT MATTERS

This session offers a unique opportunity to give kids text choices. The texts must be accessible and close to kids' independent level since the support will be procedural rather than text-specific.

For modeling, select a text on a topic you are genuinely interested in that is also accessible to students. Articles such as "Totem Poles, Family Stories," "Where in the United States Do Tornadoes Mostly Happen?" and "Where is Tornado Alley?" in *Keep Reading* have enough information to spur kids' questions and reactions.

SESSION GOALS

We want students to:

- react and respond as they read and learn information.
- sort and organize thinking on the *I Learned/I Wonder/Wow* anchor chart and thinksheet.

CONSIDERATIONS FOR PLANNING

Young readers are naturally curious. This session builds on that curiosity and adds the dimension of support in helping kids respond and react to the information they are learning. Kids learn to record, sort, and organize the information gleaned in their reading.

We show students how to take notes and organize them on an *I Learned/ I Wonder/Wow* anchor chart. Then students read independently and take notes on Post-its. At the end of the session, they organize their Post-its on an *I Learned/I Wonder/Wow* thinksheet.

Students will need Post-its and *I Learned/I Wonder/Wow* charts.

Build Background, Word and Concept Knowledge

- **Introduce the chart** and explain how it works. We use the *I Learned/I Wonder/Wow* chart to teach kids how to classify their thinking as they read: things they learn (new information), things they wonder about (questions), and their reactions (responses).

- **Show kids how to categorize** their notes to give them agency and control of the text. We want readers to see that they are in charge of the text!

. . . We are going to learn something very useful today. We are going to learn to take notes as we read *and* also record what we learn, what we wonder, and our reactions to new information.

. . . We will use a chart with three columns: *I Learned/I Wonder/Wow!* Let's investigate how it works. We read nonfiction to learn interesting facts and new information. We will record information in the first column.

. . . When we are reading nonfiction, we often have questions. Some are answered in the text, and others we are still wondering about when we finish. Our questions will go in the second column.

. . . Finally, the third column is where we put our reactions. That's where we record what our inner voice says, such as, "Wow!" "Amazing!" "Interesting!" We tap our feelings about the information as well as how it affects our background knowledge. We are always growing as we read!

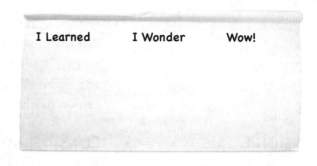

I Learned	I Wonder	Wow!

Teach/Model

- **Preview the text** together. Invite kids to share what they notice and activate their background knowledge about the topic. Preview pertinent vocabulary.

- Begin to read the text you selected, and **model how you use the chart.** Tell kids what they will be doing on their charts.

- Explain that **kids will take notes on Post-its** as they read. Later, they will sort the Post-its using their own chart.

> **Teaching Tip**
>
> Using the chart helps kids see the ways in which we categorize our thinking as we read. Consider extending this strategy to other subject areas so kids see this as a useful way to think about what they read.

. . . Let's preview the book (or article) together. What do you notice? Let's talk about some words you need to know . . .

. . . I'll use this text to show you how the chart works. As I read, I am going to write facts in the first column and questions in the next one. I'll record my reactions in the final column. (Model how you read and record, thinking aloud about how you are deciding where each should go.)

I Learned	I Wonder	Wow!
(record facts)	(record questions)	(record reactions, responses)

. . . What do you notice I do as I read? Turn and talk.

. . . You will take notes on Post-its as you read. Then, later, I'll give you a small version of the chart just like we have been using. (Show the chart so that kids see it is the same as the one on which you recorded.) We will see how we can sort the Post-its using your thinksheets.

. . . Let's be sure we are all clear on what we are doing. You'll write notes on Post-its about things you learn, things you wonder, and "Wow!" reactions and responses. One last direction: Be sure to put only one note per Post-it!

Guide/Support Practice

- **Have kids select a text** to read. Consider giving a very quick booktalk about each text to add interest. Make sure students choose a text at an appropriate level. Because engaging kids' personal interest is important, we want them to select a text they will be successful reading.

- **Scaffold students** as they use Post-its to record information as they read.

. . . Now it's your turn. Look through the books (or articles) I have gathered, and find one that interests you. (Help students select a text that catches their interest and is accessible.)

. . . It looks like you have all selected a book (article), and you have Post-its. Let's get started reading and taking notes.

. . . I will be around to listen and help you.

Wrap Up

- Invite students to **share their Post-its.**

- Give kids the chart. **Ask for a volunteer** to model the sorting process while you coach.

- **Have kids sort their Post-its** on their charts. Some students may have difficulty sorting ideas and information correctly. Support kids by reviewing the difference between a fact, a question, and a response.

- **For the next session,** students will need their charts.

. . . Let's hear what you've written on your Post-its.

. . . Now I am going to give you a thinksheet just like our chart. Let's see how we can sort the Post-its into the three categories.

. . . Would someone like to try it first, and we can all learn how to do it along with you? (Have one student spread out Post-its and start sorting while you coach. This demonstration will help kids be more successful.)

. . . Now you can try it.

. . . We'll save your charts for the next time we meet.

ASSESS AND PLAN

Did some students have difficulty sorting ideas into the three categories?

Students may need additional modeling and coaching as they try this. Because they are integrating several procedural and cognitive strategies, more practice is recommended. Consider giving children more time and support for sorting their notes on the chart before beginning Session 18b.

Did some students have difficulty handling three categories?

If students found the task too challenging, consider more practice with just one or two categories. It is very important they see the difference between facts, questions, and responses or reactions. You can offer more guided practice in each category and then integrate them into one task after kids have more experience.

While knowing research-based strategies is useful, don't forget to rely on what you do as a reader.
(Routman, 2003)

Think Across Categories of Information

This session picks up where the previous one leaves off. Students practice thinking across the three categories on their *I Learned/ I Wonder/Wow* charts.

Companion to . . .

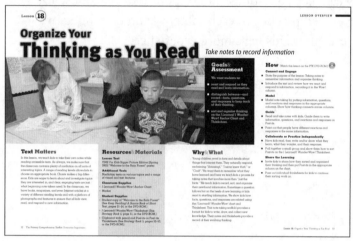

The Primary Comprehension Toolkit
Lesson 18: Organize Your Thinking as You Read

TEXT MATTERS

Students will use books and charts from the previous session.

CONSIDERATIONS FOR PLANNING

In the previous session, kids recorded, sorted, and organized information from their reading. We showed students how they could take notes as they read, using Post-its to record and a thinksheet—*I Learned/I Wonder/Wow!*— to sort their ideas into three categories.

Students will need their Post-its and thinksheets from the previous session.

In this session, we focus on helping kids think across the three categories. We help them discover that what they learn leads to wondering, and wondering leads to answers and reactions and responses.

SESSION GOALS

We want students to:

- react and respond as they read and learn information.

- sort and organize thinking on the *I Learned/I Wonder/ Wow* anchor chart and thinksheet.

Build Background, Word and Concept Knowledge

TEACHING MOVES

- **Remind kids** that they are learning to take notes.

- **Review with kids** what they did in the previous session.

- **Have kids share** some of the Post-its they put on their *I Learned/I Wonder/Wow* charts.

TEACHING LANGUAGE

. . . Last time, you learned something really important—something you will use FOREVER! You learned to take notes!

. . . Who can help us remember what we did last time? That's right! We read, took notes, and then sorted the Post-its we wrote on a chart with three columns: *I Learned/I Wonder/Wow.*

. . . Let's look at some of the Post-its you put on your chart. (Review quickly.)

Teach/Model

- Review your own chart to **make connections** among the three columns. This helps kids see that thinking creates more thinking and reactions and responses to our learning and our wondering.

- Show kids how you sometimes go back to the text and **reread to clarify.**

- Model how you **use arrows to show connections** across the columns.

. . . I want to show you something very cool. Remember, the text I was reading was . . . I took notes on Post-its as I read.

. . . Remember I used the chart to record my notes, writing them in one of the three columns.

. . . I'm going to look back over the chart I made to see how what I learned often leads to responses and reactions, and how learning something new sometimes creates another question—something I wonder about.

I Learned	I Wonder	Wow!
(record facts)	(record questions)	(record reactions, responses)

. . . I can connect my thinking across the categories with arrows. For instance, I can show how I answered one of my questions by drawing an arrow from my question to the information that answers it. (Model how you think and draw arrows to make connections.)

. . . Sometimes I need to look back at the text to reread and clarify my thinking. (Model how you check something in the text.)

Guide/Support Practice

- **Have kids look for connections** on their charts. Have them draw arrows to connect ideas.

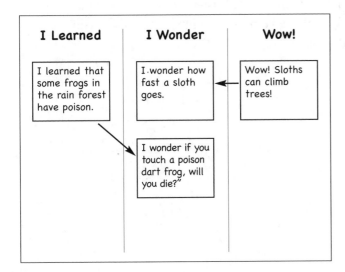

I Learned	I Wonder	Wow!
I learned that some frogs in the rain forest have poison.	I wonder how fast a sloth goes.	Wow! Sloths can climb trees!
	I wonder if you touch a poison dart frog, will you die?"	

- Invite students to **share some examples.**

- **Scaffold kids' thinking** as they look for connections across the three categories.

. . . Now look at your own charts. What connections do you see? Maybe something you learned made you ask a question. Or maybe you found the answer to one of your questions. Draw arrows to show the connections you see.

. . . Who wants to tell us how you can connect your thinking across the categories? (Have kids share examples from their own charts.)

. . . Turn and talk. Share your charts and how your thinking connects across the categories.

. . . I will be around to listen and help you.

Wrap Up

- **Review what kids learned.** We want kids to learn that thinking deeply always creates more thinking. They do this naturally as young children when they are genuinely curious about something. We want to harness that same thinking and help kids put it to use in the classroom.

. . . What did you learn today?

. . . Good thinking! You learned that by taking notes and keeping track of your learning, questions, and reactions, you can remember important information!

ASSESS AND PLAN

Did some students have difficulty taking notes and seeing connections among the categories?

Kids need multiple opportunities to learn. They learn best when we model and then support them. Have kids read additional books that interest them, and invite them to use Post-its and the *I Learned/I Wonder/Wow* thinksheet. Make time to confer with kids so you can coach them individually.

Reading Conference
Determine Importance

After this unit, you want to know that students are sorting and sifting information to remember the most important ideas and are able to put information into their own words as they learn it. Your conference should help the student use several different approaches to determining importance and organizing information.

1. **Invite the student to choose a passage and create a context for it.**
   - Choose a part of your book to read to me.
   - Tell me what it's about.
   - Tell me about the most important information you read about.

2. **Focus on how the student sorted out important information and details.**
   - Share the important information in what you read. Now share some details. How did you figure out what was important and what was a detail?

3. **Focus on paraphrasing information.**
   - Now that you read this part, take a minute and think about it. Now try to put what you learned into your own words.
   - Share any reactions or responses you had to this part.

4. **Focus on how the student organizes thinking.**
   - Let's talk about how you organized your thinking as you read this. First, tell me what you learned. Next, what do you wonder (what are your questions) about this new information? Finally, what are your reactions and responses to this information?
   - Talk about how you connected your thinking. Did you answer any of your questions? Did your reactions lead to any new questions?

Reading Conference Recording Form: Determine Importance

Name _____   Date _____

Book title _____

GOAL The student . . .	EVIDENCE This student . . .
1. Understands the text • Tells what the book is about and the most important things he or she learned from it	
2. Can tell the difference between important information and details • Relates important information and details • Explains how he or she distinguished between important information and details	
3. Puts new information into her or his own words to paraphrase it • Describes what he or she learned in his or her own words • Shares personal response	
4. Organizes thinking • Tells what he or she learned, questioned, and responded to • Explains how she or he connected facts, questions, and responses	Note: You may also want to review the student's *I Learned/I Wonder/Wow* thinksheet to evaluate thinking organization.

©2010 by Stephanie Harvey, Anne Goudvis, and Judy Wallis. From *Comprehension Intervention: Small-Group Lessons for The Primary Comprehension Toolkit*. Portsmouth, NH: Heinemann. This page may be copied for classroom use only.

Conference Recording Form for "Determine Importance," located in "Resources" section.

Follow-Ups

If the student has difficulty with any of the primary goals in this unit, prompts like the following may be helpful during independent work in subsequent units.

- Tell me about the important information.
- Share any questions or responses you have to this information.
- Did you keep the difference between interesting details and important information in mind as you read?
- Try putting that into your own words. Think about what the text is saying first; then think about how you could say it.
- Tell me how you figured out the facts. Tell me what you learned.
- Tell me about your questions.
- Tell me about your responses.

Language students may use to demonstrate
that they are identifying important information.

- . . . is important information. . . . is a detail!
- This is important to remember.
- I think this means . . .
- The book (article, etc.) is saying . . . (paraphrases)
- This what I learned (facts) . . . These are my questions . . . . These are my responses . . .
- I think the big idea is . . .

Summarize and Synthesize

Synthesizing information nudges readers to see the "big picture." It pulls together their thinking. It's not enough for readers simply to recall or restate the facts. They need to use a variety of comprehension strategies, including asking questions, inferring, and determining what's important, to understand big ideas. They merge new information with what they already know and construct meaning as they go. As they distill nonfiction text into a few important ideas, they make the information their own. In *The Primary Comprehension Toolkit*, children summarize and synthesize their thinking by drawing and writing in all sorts of original ways: creating poems, posters, and other projects that demonstrate their learning and understanding. These sessions help prime students for the whole-class investigation in Toolkit Lessons 21 and 22.

If the text is too short, there may be nothing of substance to summarize. However, if the text is too long, students may be unable to perform all of the summarizing processes needed. (Guthrie, Wigfield, and Perencevich, 2004)

Companion to ...

The Primary Comprehension Toolkit
Lesson 19: Summarize Information

SESSION GOAL

We want students to:

- understand that summarizing information about a topic helps us learn and remember important information (nonfiction).

Summarize During Reading

In *The Primary Comprehension Toolkit* Lesson 19, students learn to write a developmentally appropriate summary by rereading their notes, combining information and thinking, and organizing their ideas in response to a read-aloud article. The two sessions supporting Lesson 19 help kids break down this process. In this first session, they focus on summarizing and paraphrasing information while they are reading another article.

TEXT MATTERS

Select a text that has "just enough" information for kids to summarize. Short books or articles with headings that organize information in chunks are good choices. The text structure assists kids and shows them that summarizing is as much a "during reading" process as it is an "after reading" process.

Ladybugs by Monica Hughes and *Coral Reef Animals* by Francine Galko are short and well organized. "Prairie Dog Homes," "The Three Goats," and "Ask the Farmer!" in *Keep Reading* and "Slithering Snakes" in *Toolkit Texts: Grades 2–3* have headings that help kids summarize during reading.

CONSIDERATIONS FOR PLANNING

Summarizing is a powerful tool for readers, writers, listeners, and speakers. It helps us form well-crafted "gist" statements that capture the essence of a text. Summarizing has typically been treated as an "after reading" activity. By teaching kids to summarize *during and after* reading, we show them how to keep track of information as they read. Summarizing as they read makes the task of creating a whole-text summary much more manageable.

In this session we focus on the "thinking work" involved in summarizing during reading. In the next session we teach kids how to compose a whole-text summary.

Students will need Post-its.

Build Background, Word and Concept Knowledge

- **Discuss what *summarizing* is.** In this session, we teach kids how to summarize as they are reading. Summarizing draws from other strategies we have taught kids, especially determining importance.

- **Introduce the term *gist*.**

- Help students understand the **difference between a *topic* and a *summary*:**

  Topic = the subject of something we are reading or talking about

  Summary = what we know about a topic

. . . When we are listening or reading something, I often say to you, "Who can help summarize that?" What does that mean? Turn and talk.

. . . Right! To *summarize* is to "capture" all the important parts of a spoken or written message. We sometimes call this "getting the *gist*."

. . . When we read, the text is about *something*—a topic. For example, if I want to learn more about dogs, the topic I read about is "dogs." When we create a summary about dogs, we are pulling together important information about dogs so we can share it.

. . . Today we will learn how to create a summary.

Teach/Model

- **Preview the text.** We teach kids to think about the topic and then how to summarize as they read. Introduce pertinent vocabulary.

- Model how you **summarize as you read.** In an article, write a Post-it for each "chunk" (paragraph or section) within the article. In a book, use a Post-it for each page or two. Show students how you note just the most important information in each section.

- Reinforce the **importance of** *paraphrasing.* When we summarize, we often shorten the "gist" or key ideas into brief phrases that we will combine into the final summary. When kids put information into their own words and language, we know they really understand it.

. . . I have an interesting text for us to read! Let's look at it. What do you think the topic is?

. . . There are a few words you will need to know. Here's one . . .

. . . So now we know the topic, and we will read to find out more about that topic. Then we can create a summary of what we learn about (topic).

. . . I want to show you how I keep track of important information as I read. I'll use Post-its. Then, when I finish reading, I'll look back at my Post-its to help me write my summary.

. . . Here is how it works. (Read the first part of the text.) Let's see if I can summarize this. I'm going to paraphrase—put this information in my own words. I'll write this on a Post-it. I'm careful not to write too much, just the most important information.

. . . Now let's read this part. (Read another paragraph or section and demonstrate paraphrasing again.)

Guide/Support Practice

- Prompt kids to **summarize their task.** Make sure students understand the process and purpose of putting Post-its on each page or section to create micro-summaries.

- **Have kids read** and use Post-its to summarize as they read.

- **Scaffold students** as needed. Some kids may need an oral rehearsal before writing. If you see students having difficulty, ask them to say it first before writing it.

. . . Now it's your turn. Who can *summarize* our task? (Guide kids to say how they will read the information, think about it, and put it in their own words.)

. . . Let's get started reading. Everyone has Post-its. Use them to summarize the most important information as you read. Remember to put it in your own words.

. . . I will be around to listen and help you.

Wrap Up

- Have kids **share their Post-its.** If students have not completed the text, have them share what they have done thus far.

- **Look for "gist."** If kids are not capturing the important information and putting it in their own words, you may need to review and model more before moving on to the next session.

- **For the next session,** have kids keep their Post-its in their texts.

. . . Great! I see you've written some important information in your own words on the Post-its.

. . . Let's share a few of the Post-its you wrote. Be sure to tell us what part your Post-it summarizes.

. . . What great thinking today! Next, we'll use your Post-its to create a summary of the whole text! So leave your Post-its in your texts for our next meeting.

ASSESS AND PLAN

Did some students have difficulty recording ideas as paraphrases?
Paraphrasing and using short phrases to capture ideas can be challenging tasks. Students may need additional modeling and coaching as they put the text's ideas into their own words. Consider conferring with kids individually to provide more support as they put information in their own words and jot down their "paraphrasing" themselves.

Summarizing . . . is the ability to delete irrelevant details, combine similar ideas, condense main ideas, and connect major themes into concise statements that capture the purpose of a reading. (Mandel, Gambrell, and Pressley, 2003)

Companion to . . .

The Primary Comprehension Toolkit
Lesson 19: Summarize Information

SESSION GOALS

We want students to:

- understand that summarizing information about a topic helps us learn and remember important information (nonfiction).
- use reading, writing, and thinking strategies to create a developmentally appropriate summary.
- merge their thinking with the information to write a summary that is interesting to read and written in authentic voice.

Summarize After Reading

This session builds on the previous one. Students use the Post-its they wrote during reading to create a summary after reading.

TEXT MATTERS

Have kids use the text from the previous session. If they have not finished the text, have them complete the reading before going on to this session.

CONSIDERATIONS FOR PLANNING

In this session, kids use the Post-its from their reading to create a written summary. Talking is an important part of teaching summarizing. Oral rehearsal helps kids decide what they will say about their topic before recording their thinking. Then writing the summary flows much more naturally.

Students have already put information into their own words, without telling too much, and have written their thinking on Post-its. We use the Post-its created in the previous session to write a summary. We model how we think about and compose a summary orally, and then we demonstrate how we write it.

Be prepared to post a copy of the *How to Create a Summary* anchor chart used in this session. (See Teach/Model.)

You will need your text with Post-its from the previous session.

Students will need their texts with Post-its.

Consider having students use dry erase boards to draft their summaries.

Build Background, Word and Concept Knowledge

- **Help kids review** what they know about summarizing.

- Have kids **share their Post-its** from the previous session. If they haven't finished reading the text, this will serve as a review and an opportunity for another quick demonstration.

- **If kids have not finished** reading, allow time to finish before teaching them how to write a summary.

. . . We've been talking about summarizing. Turn and talk about what you know.

. . . Good thinking. When we summarize, we think about the important information in a text—ideas we want to remember and tell someone about.

. . . While you were reading last time, you wrote down your information in your own words on Post-its. Let's look at some of them.

. . . Today you will learn to write a summary using your Post-its. (If kids haven't finished reading the text and paraphrasing the "gist" on Post-its, have them finish the text before continuing.)

Teach/Model

■ **Read the anchor chart,** "How to Create a Summary." This comes from *The Primary Comprehension Toolkit* Lesson 19. Posting it reminds kids of the sequence of steps important to writing.

How to Create a Summary

1. Reread your notes on the topic. Make sure they are accurate and in your own words.

2. Think about the topic and the information that tells about it.

3. Put the notes in order—what comes first, second, third, etc.

4. Remember to tell what is impor-tant, but don't tell too much.

■ **Use your own Post-its** to show students how you get ready to write a summary.

■ Model how you **check your Post-its for accuracy.**

■ Model how you **delete and combine ideas.** We show kids that summarizing is about prac-ticing the art of deletion! A summary is *not* a retelling; it is the gist, essence, and most important ideas in the text.

■ Model how you **put your Post-its in order.** As you sort your Post-its, consider and talk about how the summary might be affected. Text structure determines how we write a summary. For example, if the text is chronological, the summary will also be arranged in chronological order.

. . . Let's review the steps of writing a summary on our anchor chart.

. . . Now we'll read and organize my Post-its to get ready to write our summary.

. . . Let's look at my Post-its. (Read through your Post-its so kids hear and see the information and ideas you have recorded.)

. . . We need to check the information I recorded. (Check each Post-it against the text.) Yes, it makes sense, and it's in my own words.

. . . I am going to take off my Post-its now and lay them out so we can read them. Each one is a mini-summary of one part of the text.

. . . Let's see if there are any ideas I can combine. (Read through the Post-its and look for ways to combine ideas that are similar.)

. . . Next, I need to think about how to order my summary. Let's think about what to write first, and second, and so on. We can put the Post-its in that order. (Go back to the text and look at the way the text is written. Think aloud about how best to order your summary.)

. . . Last but not least, we'll write our summary and try to make it really interesting. Let me show you how I use my Post-its to do that. (Model writing the summary.)

Guide/Support Practice

- Have kids **plan and write their summaries.** Make sure kids understand the process.

- **Scaffold students** as they use their Post-its to create their own summaries. Some kids may need an oral rehearsal before writing. Have kids summarize orally with one another before they write.

- **Dry erase boards** may be used to draft and ease revisions.

. . . Now it's your turn. Lift your Post-its from the text and lay them out so you can see them.

. . . Look for information you can combine into one sentence, like this. (Refer back to model.)

. . . Think about the order you will put your Post-its in.

. . . Take a moment to talk through your summary before you write. Remember to make it interesting! (Have kids turn and talk, then write. Move about the group to support each student.)

Wrap Up

- Have kids **share their summaries.**

. . . Let's read our summaries.

. . . You did a great job!

ASSESS AND PLAN

Did some students have difficulty creating their summaries?
Consider using the *How to Create a Summary* anchor chart as a "rubric" to help kids assess the process and their resulting summaries. Students will grow in their ability to summarize. Continue to model and coach summarizing and paraphrasing as kids read other texts.

> *Theme in literature is the idea that holds the story together, such as a comment about either society, human nature, or the human condition.* (Lehr, 1991)

Synthesize Big Ideas from Fiction

In *The Primary Comprehension Toolkit* Lesson 20, students learn to synthesize big ideas from fiction as they respond to a read-aloud story that contains a lot of information. This session gives students the opportunity to practice synthesizing big ideas from fiction as they read another story.

TEXT MATTERS

Sharing texts that offer a range of genres and topics is one of the ways we teach young readers to gain flexibility and discover that, though they encounter diversity, they have the ability to navigate to meaning.

Companion to . . .

The Primary Comprehension Toolkit
Lesson 20: Read to Get the Big Ideas

Excellent selections for this session are short, well-written stories that have an informational strand as well as a storyline that carries the information. A short article also works. "How Seeds Spread" and "Footprints in the Forest" in *Keep Reading* have story qualities as well as information from which kids can synthesize big ideas.

CONSIDERATIONS FOR PLANNING

This session offers students an opportunity to explore fiction. In addition to developing an appreciation of the story, we want kids to be sensitive to and synthesize the ideas and issues in the story. Students will utilize many previously learned strategies—inferring, visualizing, and questioning—as they move into and "live inside" the story.

In this session, we help kids come to appreciate the ideas that may be embedded within a story. They synthesize the big ideas or themes of the story as well as appreciate the new information they learn during reading.

Students will need Post-its.

SESSION GOALS

We want students to:

- understand important ideas from a character's words and actions as well as from story events.
- synthesize big ideas from fiction using several strategies, especially inferring, visualizing, and connecting.
- construct important ideas based on content information.

Build Background, Word and Concept Knowledge

- **Prepare kids to read a story.** Students read fiction in this session. Since this is a departure from most texts they have been reading, we explain the difference between fiction and nonfiction. Though we often group texts into these categories, the range within each category is immense.

- **Talk about the strategies** kids will use. The type of fiction we use for this session both tells a story and offers kids information and something to think about. Grasping the "themes" or big ideas of a story allows kids to synthesize the story and consider the big ideas.

. . . Today we are going to read a story. What does that word *story* mean? Turn and talk.

. . . Right! A story tells about something or someone. Some stories are believable because they capture realistic things that could happen. Some stories could never happen in real life. But all stories have characters and events that we have to really think about. Sometimes we ask questions, infer, or visualize as we listen to a story. We use all our reading strategies to understand it.

Teach/Model

- **Introduce the story** and have kids share what they notice about the cover (or first page of the article).

- **Read the beginning.** Model how you think about the story. We teach kids to use three different strategies so that they can begin to synthesize from the story as they read. We support them to question, infer, and visualize about the characters and events in the story to arrive at some of the big ideas, themes, or messages.

- **Model how you use Post-its** to keep track of your thinking.

> **Teaching Tip**
>
> Stories call upon kids' imagination. They slip into stories with ease. In this session, not only do we want young readers to enjoy the story, we also want them to visualize, infer, and question to better understand the story and surface the themes, big ideas, or messages.

. . . I have selected a wonderful story for us today. (Show the cover and read the title.)

. . . Turn and talk about what you notice about the cover—both the picture and the title.

. . . I'm going to read you a page or two (or paragraph or section of the article).

. . . Let's think about the characters. What can you infer about their actions—what they do and what they say? What do you wonder about this character? (Model how you use strategy language—*I think, I wonder, I infer, I visualize*—to understand the characters and events.)

. . . Let's keep track of our thinking on Post-its as we read on. (Model how you keep track of the characters and events of the story.)

. . . I'm starting to understand a big idea here . . . . (Model how you are arriving at a big idea or theme.) I think the big idea is that . . . .

Guide/Support Practice

TEACHING MOVES

- **Have students read.** Remind them to jot or draw their thinking on Post-its as they read. These will be used to help them synthesize and summarize the story.

- **Scaffold students** as they use Post-its to track the events of the story and the growing synthesis of what the story is about.

TEACHING LANGUAGE

. . . Now you will read on. Everyone has Post-its so you can jot down or draw your thinking.

. . . I will be around to listen and help. (Encourage kids to use language such as "I think this story is about . . . ," "I infer a big idea is . . . ," or "The message is . . . .")

Wrap Up

TEACHING MOVES

- Have kids **share their Post-its.** Check to be sure kids are synthesizing as they go—linking the story's events, characters' actions, and important ideas into the theme.

- **Help students synthesize** the big ideas in the story. Invite them to synthesize orally first. Then have them write and draw their synthesis.

TEACHING LANGUAGE

. . . Let's share a few of the Post-its you wrote. Be sure to tell us what part you were reading when you wrote the Post-it.

. . . Let's synthesize, or put the ideas all together. One way to do that is to consider this question: If you could only use a few words to tell about the story, what would your words be?

. . . Write down your words on a piece of paper. When you leave, you'll take your papers with you and add a drawing that shows what the story is all about—how you synthesize the big ideas in the story.

ASSESS AND PLAN

Did students have difficulty linking big ideas across the story?
Synthesizing the big ideas into a whole is challenging. It helps some students if we ask them what *one* word comes to mind after reading the text. Often the word is the theme.

Did students integrate their previously learned skills into synthesizing?
Kids will generally use the language of thinking as they discuss the story and read. If you don't hear language such as "I inferred . . . ," "I visualized . . . ," and "I think . . . ," provide more modeling in read-aloud and discussions. Kids can help each other, too, by offering a high five or thumbs up when they hear others use thinking language.

Reading Conference

Summarize and Synthesize

After this unit, you want to know that students are able to synthesize information and come up with the big ideas to create a summary, so your conference will prompt the student to summarize and explain the process.

1. **Invite the student to choose a passage and tell what the whole book or article is about.**
   - Choose a part of your text and read it to me.
   - Tell me what your book (or article) is about in just one or two sentences.

2. **Ask the student to summarize what he or she just read.**
   - Summarize what you've read for me. Tell me in your own words.
   - Is that an important part of the story (book, article)? How did you decide what was important?
   - What do you think of what you've read? What do you want to remember about it?

3. **Focus on the student's ability to synthesize and come up with the big ideas in text.**
   - (*If reading fiction*) What big ideas did you come up with for your book? What did the characters say and do that helped you figure that out?
   - (*If reading nonfiction*) What big ideas did you come up with for your book? What facts did you put together with your own thinking to come up with a bigger idea?

Reading Conference Recording Form: Summarize and Synthesize
Name _____ Date _____
Book title _____

GOAL	EVIDENCE
The student . . .	This student . . .
1. Understands the text • Tells about the passage he or she read without telling too much	
2. Puts information into his or her own words to summarize the text • Retells facts from the text in her or his own words • Includes important information that she or he wants to remember	
3. Comes up with the big ideas • (If reading fiction) Uses characters and events to come up with big ideas • (If reading nonfiction) Comes up with big ideas by merging thinking with the information	

©2010 by Stephanie Harvey, Anne Goudvis, and Judy Wallis. From *Comprehension Intervention: Small-Group Lessons for The Primary Comprehension Toolkit.* Portsmouth, NH: Heinemann. This page may be copied for classroom use only.

Conference Recording Form for "Summarize and Synthesize," located in "Resources" section.

Language students may use to demonstrate that they are summarizing and synthesizing the information

- The big idea here is . . .
- This is really important . . .
- A new idea I had here was . . .
- I used to think . . . , but now I think . . .

Follow-Ups

If the student has difficulty with any of the primary goals in this unit, prompts like the following may be helpful during independent work in subsequent units.

- Did you remember to stop and think frequently as you were reading?
- Did you put the information into your own words?
- What do you think are some of the big ideas here?
- Did any new ideas pop into your head as you were reading?

Resources

Reading Conference Recording Forms

Monitor Comprehension

Activate and Connect

Ask Questions

Infer and Visualize

Determine Importance

Summarize and Synthesize

Reading Conference Recording Form: Monitor Comprehension

Name _____   Date _____

Book title _____

GOAL	EVIDENCE
The student . . .	**This student . . .**
1. Understands the text • Tells what the book is about and talks about what she or he was thinking while reading	
2. Is aware of what he or she thinks about the text • Writes or draws something about the text • Talks about what the text makes him or her think or wonder about • Talks about what the text reminds him or her of	
3. (If reading nonfiction with features) Knows about text and visual features and their purposes • Names text and visual features • Shares information learned from text and visual features • Explains the purpose of a feature	

©2010 by Stephanie Harvey, Anne Goudvis, and Judy Wallis. From *Comprehension Intervention: Small-Group Lessons for The Primary Comprehension Toolkit*. Portsmouth, NH: Heinemann. This page may be copied for classroom use only.

Reading Conference Recording Form: Activate and Connect

Name _____ Date _____

Book title _____

GOAL	EVIDENCE
The student . . .	**This student . . .**
1. Understands the text • Tells what the book is about	
2. (If reading fiction) Uses connections to understand text • Makes connections to personal experience • Describes how connections furthered understanding of the text	
3. (If reading nonfiction) Activates background knowledge to understand new information • Notices and reacts when she or he learns something new • Relates background knowledge to new learning	
4. Shares teaching book • Enthusiastically shares information, visual and text features	

©2010 by Stephanie Harvey, Anne Goudvis, and Judy Wallis. From *Comprehension Intervention: Small-Group Lessons for The Primary Comprehension Toolkit*. Portsmouth, NH: Heinemann. This page may be copied for classroom use only.

Reading Conference Recording Form: Ask Questions

Name _____ Date _____

Book title _____

GOAL	EVIDENCE
The student . . .	**This student . . .**
1. Understands and questions the text • Tells what the text is about and asks questions about it	
2. Asks questions about new learning • Stops to ask a question to express curiosity about new learning	
3. Reads with a question in mind and uses strategies to answer it • To find answers: – reads on – uses pictures – uses text features • Recognizes that not all questions are answered	

©2010 by Stephanie Harvey, Anne Goudvis, and Judy Wallis. From *Comprehension Intervention: Small-Group Lessons for The Primary Comprehension Toolkit*. Portsmouth, NH: Heinemann. This page may be copied for classroom use only.

Reading Conference Recording Form: Infer and Visualize

Name _____   Date _____

Book title _____

GOAL	EVIDENCE
The student . . .	**This student . . .**
1. Understands the text • Tells what the book is about and talks about what he or she was visualizing and inferring while reading	
2. (If reading fiction or poetry) Is aware of her or his own visualizing and inferring strategies • Describes and explains inferences and mental images that enhance the meaning of the text • Makes inferences to predict what is going to happen next	
3. Infers and visualizes to make sense of information • Combines text clues with background knowledge to understand part of the text • (If reading nonfiction with features) Infers information from features • Visualizes information from the text	

©2010 by Stephanie Harvey, Anne Goudvis, and Judy Wallis. From *Comprehension Intervention: Small-Group Lessons for The Primary Comprehension Toolkit.* Portsmouth, NH: Heinemann. This page may be copied for classroom use only.

Reading Conference Recording Form: Determine Importance

Name _____   Date _____

Book title _____

GOAL	EVIDENCE
The student . . .	**This student . . .**
1. Understands the text • Tells what the book is about and the most important things he or she learned from it	
2. Can tell the difference between important information and details • Relates important information and details • Explains how he or she distinguished between important information and details	
3. Puts new information into her or his own words to paraphrase it • Describes what he or she learned in his or her own words • Shares personal response	
4. Organizes thinking • Tells what he or she learned, questioned, and responded to • Explains how she or he connected facts, questions, and responses	Note: You may also want to review the student's *I Learned/I Wonder/ Wow* thinksheet to evaluate thinking organization.

©2010 by Stephanie Harvey, Anne Goudvis, and Judy Wallis. From *Comprehension Intervention: Small-Group Lessons for The Primary Comprehension Toolkit*. Portsmouth, NH: Heinemann. This page may be copied for classroom use only.

Reading Conference Recording Form: Summarize and Synthesize

Name _____   Date _____

Book title _____

GOAL	EVIDENCE
The student . . .	**This student . . .**
1. Understands the text • Tells about the passage he or she read without telling too much	
2. Puts information into his or her own words to summarize the text • Retells facts from the text in her or his own words • Includes important information that she or he wants to remember	
3. Comes up with the big ideas • (If reading fiction) Uses characters and events to come up with big ideas • (If reading nonfiction) Comes up with big ideas by merging thinking with the information	

©2010 by Stephanie Harvey, Anne Goudvis, and Judy Wallis. From *Comprehension Intervention: Small-Group Lessons for The Primary Comprehension Toolkit*. Portsmouth, NH: Heinemann. This page may be copied for classroom use only.